HONEY FOR A
child's heart

Also by Gladys Hunt

Honey for a Teen's Heart (with Barbara Hampton)
Honey for a Woman's Heart

HONEY FOR A
child's heart

The Imaginative Use of Books in Family Life

Fourth Edition

Gladys Hunt

ZONDERVAN™

GRAND RAPIDS, MICHIGAN 49530 USA

ZONDERVAN™

Honey for a Child's Heart

Copyright © 1969, 1978, 1989, 2002 by Gladys M. Hunt

Requests for information should be addressed to:

Zondervan, *Grand Rapids, Michigan 49530*

Library of Congress Cataloging-in-Publication Data

Hunt, Gladys M.
    Honey for a child's heart : the imaginative use of books in family life / Gladys Hunt. — 4th ed.
       p. cm.
  Includes bibliographical references.
    ISBN 0-310-24246-0 (Softcover)
    1. Children — Books and reading.   2. Children — Religious life.   I. Title.
  Z1037 .H945 2001
  028'.9 — dc21

2001007850

Interior design by Beth Shagene

Printed in the United States of America

11 12 13 14 15 /DCI/ 40 39 38 37 36 35 34 33 32 31 30 29 28 27 26 25

To Mark and Keith,
with love and thanks
for many happy hours of reading together

Contents

Acknowledgments

Do you know how many children's books are now published each year? It's overwhelming! The Horn Book Guide reviews about 4,700 books every year, and that only scratches the surface of what is being published. More than a thousand of these are picture books—and only a fraction of those published are reviewed and annotated. How does a person keep track of all these books?

First, you read and read and read. Second, you look for others who are eager to help. Many of these—friends, family members, librarians, readers, both young and older—gave me lists of their favorite books, often saying, "You must include this one!" Many of these books subsequently found their way into my booklist.

My thanks go to many young friends and their families who shared book titles with me—Leah Latterner, the Kolk boys, Clara Schriemer, Daniel Schriemer, Jonathan White, the Hollenbeck girls, and others. Librarians like Kristy Motz and Daryl Marks gave me suggestions from their expertise. Alyce t. Reimer loves picture books and gave me a list of her favorites. Sarah Feldhake, a thoughtful book-loving teen, evaluated and annotated a number of books for readers nine and older. My thanks to all of these—and anyone else who ever gave me a book recommendation.

Mostly I think we all owe a sincere voice of appreciation to the imaginative authors/illustrators who bring us wonderful reading experiences and enjoyment of books.

A final note of thanks to Sandra Vander Zicht at Zondervan who encouraged this updated version, giving me an opportunity to share more good books and the new things I have been learning. Special thanks to Angela Scheff, who did the final editing, and to Beth Shagene, the designer of the book.

You may have tangible wealth untold,
Caskets of jewels and coffers of gold;
Richer than I you can never be
I had parents who read to me.

S. GILLILAND

Foreword

Dear Gladys Hunt,

My mother, a missionary to Chile with five children, is one of your most avid fans. The first edition of *Honey for a Child's Heart* was on our shelves at home and I frequently saw Mama concentrating on some nugget of wisdom or looking for a book in the bibliography. All I had to do was to ask for a book and she would recommend a wonderful book for me.

Then I grew up and left home. After college I realized how lost I was in libraries without my mother. Then you wrote your book for teens, a book that I have read and reread, both in order to find good books for myself, as well as to recommend them to others. I am a high school English teacher, fascinated by the world of books and eager to encourage others to enjoy all that books have to offer.

My focus changed recently when I discovered that my husband and I are expecting a baby. This monumental event is due to take place in April, and I've discovered that I suddenly want to be PERFECT for this child. Since this goal probably won't be accomplished in a few months, I decided to set smaller ones dealing especially with passing on values and beliefs. One of the greatest things my parents have modeled for me has been a love of books. So I went out and bought *Honey for a Child's Heart*.

The experience of reading that book was like few others. That book in MY LIFE! I have seen it work. Everything you said about books and faith and the transmittal of values spoke Truth to me. I never knew all my mother had adopted from your book until now: reading Proverbs around the breakfast table, the question and answer time after a chapter of the Bible, and the reading aloud of excellent books, all of which my parents recognized as wise and practical ways to influence us kids. And now, as I start my own family, I yearn to be as influential in the lives of my children as my parents have been, thanks in great part to your incredible books.

My husband (who is in the process of becoming a reader) and I have had wonderful times reading aloud. I've read aloud the Narnia books, *The Bronze Bow, A Wrinkle in Time, The Robe,* and others, and he has loved them.

Thank you for your part in making my life so rich and for your ministry in my family as I was growing up. It has borne fruit.

Sincerely,
Jewel Kaste

Introduction

I began writing about families reading books together at the suggestion of our teenage son who wanted me to share with others the fun our family had with books. He said that reading books together seemed to him one of the most important things about our family life. This encouraged me to begin organizing ideas for a book. Later when he reminded me that Proverbs says, "Pleasant words are like a honeycomb, sweet to the soul and healing to the bones" (Proverbs 16:24), we came up with the title for this book.

The book ended up being a family venture with discussions about books at meals for weeks on end. "Remember when we read . . ." and "Don't forget to put this book in." Slips of paper were pulled out of jeans pockets or notebooks listing book titles remembered while in school. It was a tumble of memories every time books entered our discussion—not just the title of the book, but the plot, the characters, the remembering. I realized afresh what a rich treasure books have been in our family life. Honey, indeed!

Honey for a Child's Heart was the first of its kind. The publisher was wary about the idea of producing a book that promoted books from other publishers. He was open to my reasoning, and I credit him for taking the risk. My hesitant editor became enthusiastic when he saw that I was not only listing a wide variety of books, but also writing a philosophy of reading to widen the world of a child, to enhance family life, to introduce both children and parents to the best books. Who could have known the widespread impact of this book? Other books on this subject have followed, but this piece of "honeycomb" was the first of its kind.

This is the fourth revision of *Honey for a Child's Heart*. The book has been in print long enough to have its influence affect the second generation of children. I know the ideas in this book work, because I have seen the difference it has made in our own family, in our grandchildren, in my nieces and nephews, and in the many other children in our lives. Talking about books together has influenced their language usage, writing skills, imagination, and ability to analyze what they are reading. And almost nothing does more for family closeness than having a child read aloud some beautiful passage from a book—words too wonderful not to share with people you love.

It's been an awesome experience to see how this book has affected the family life of others. Some years after the book had been in print, I was at a summer training program for university students when a winsome, lanky college student approached me as if he knew me. He began by thanking me for making his life so rich. As I wondered what I had unwittingly done, he recounted his family story. When he was a little boy his mother bought *Honey for a Child's Heart* shortly after its publication; she insisted his father read it, and together they made a pact to be a reading family. Ben recited a long list of titles, places, or vacations where his parents and his siblings had read stories. Our conversation became more and more animated as the list of books he mentioned grew longer and longer. It was as if we knew all the same people from the stories we had read. We felt like old friends, a very special connection between us. The encounter was a gift to me, because he is part of what this book is all about.

Many mothers and fathers have thanked me "for helping us raise our children"—which is a nice way to put it since I believe books are one of the important ingredients for good family life. But letters from the children of these parents are even dearer to me. What a wonderful lot of people share this love of books with their children!

Now I've had the fun of revising and bringing *Honey for a Child's Heart* up-to-date again. This means I have books stacked everywhere, that I am always engrossed in a new one, and frequently read choice paragraphs to my husband and our grown children, showing them the imaginative illustrations that wonderfully illumine so many new books.

Many children and I share books, and I take seriously the recommendations they give me. A neighbor girl one time asked me if the piles of children's books she saw stacked around the house were mine or belonged to someone else. When she found they were mine and I was reading them, she began stopping by to share her books with me. "It isn't due at the library for three more days," she would say. "Do you have time to read it?" And you can bet that I did!

GLADYS HUNT

Part 1

Using Books to Help Children Grow

Playing Pooh sticks.

Chapter 1

Bequest of Wings

I'm going to play in the Hundred Acre Wood," said the small boy who lived at our house.

I knew what he meant and where he was going, and so I said, "Fine. If you see Owl, be sure to ask him about Eeyore's tail."

We knew about Eeyore, Pooh, Piglet, Owl, and Christopher Robin. Together we had met them in a book written by A. A. Milne, and our life would always be richer because they had become our friends. To this day I feel sorry for anyone who hasn't made their acquaintance by reading the original book.

That is what a book does. It introduces us to people and places we wouldn't ordinarily know. A good book is a magic gateway into a wider world of wonder, beauty, delight, and adventure. Books are experiences that make us grow, that add something to our inner stature.

Children and books go together in a special way. I can't imagine any pleasure greater than bringing to the uncluttered, supple mind of a child the delight of knowing the many rich things God has given us to enjoy. Parents have this wonderful privilege, and books are their keenest tools. Children don't stumble onto good books by themselves; they must be introduced to the wonder of words put together in such a way that they spin out pure joy and magic.[1]

---

[1]*Magic:* "Any extraordinary or irresistible influence." *The Random House Dictionary*.

Wonderful Words

I had an eloquent older journalism professor at the university who frequently got carried away in trying to convince his students about the marvel of words. He would exclaim rapturously, "Oh, the beauty and mystery of words! What richness can be conveyed by those who master them!" And while we youthfully mocked him as we recounted his dramatic incantations to our friends, we ourselves coveted the mastery of words, the symbols that convey ideas. We knew that what he said was true.

Take all the words available in the human vocabulary and read them from the dictionary, and you have only a list of words. But with the creativity and imagination God has given human beings, let these words flow together in the right order and they give wings to the spirit. Every child ought to know the pleasure of words so well chosen that they awaken sensibility, great emotions, and understanding of truth. This is the magic of words—a touch of the supernatural, communication that ministers to the spirit, a true gift.

We cannot underestimate the use of words in creative thought! Proverbs says, "A word fitly spoken is like apples of gold in pictures of silver." The right word in the right place is a magnificent gift. Somehow a limited, poverty-stricken vocabulary works toward equally limited use of ideas and imagination. On the other hand, the provocative use of the right words, of a growing vocabulary, gives us adequate material with which to clothe our thoughts and leads to a richer world of expression.

What fun it is to encourage a personal awareness of words in a child—the delight of sound, the color and variety of words available to our use. What a difference there is between a vocabulary drill and feeling the beauty of words. Books, the right kind of books, can give us the experience of words. They have power to evoke emotion, a sense of spiritual conviction, an inner expansion that fills a child to the brim so that "the years ahead will never run dry."

Listen to Barbara Cooney's description of winter in *Island Boy,*

> When the house had been banked with spruce boughs and the firewood cut for winter, the bitter cold came. Matthais would wake with the tip of his nose like ice. The windowpanes frosted over, and the wind whistled in the chimney. Sea smoke hung over the open water. Then the children would crowd into the steamy kitchen, learning to read and write under Ma's fierce eye.

What wonderful feelings, smells, and scenery these words give to the reader, quite apart from Cooney's sensitive pictures. The words are ordinary, but well-chosen. From stories like these children learn how to use language.

Capturing Experiences with Words

Words and experience go together. One enriches the other. I like to remember the night we stayed late after a family picnic along an isolated lake in the north woods—far past normal bedtime for children. We watched the rosy glow of the sunset color the sky on the far side of the lake and darken the silhouettes of the trees. We felt the sand shed its warmth and take on a damp coolness. And then darkness fell over our world. We sat around the campfire and listened to the night sounds. Young ears picked up things older ears hadn't heard. What we heard we tried to express in words.

Deep-voiced bullfrogs far away, anxious peepers closer by, the gentle lap of the water on the shore, the loon crying in the distance, the crackle of the wood in the fire, the sparks going upward like brief fireflies. And then, as a special gift, a whippoorwill, a shy bird usually heard only from a distance, lit in the bush just behind us and startled us with his clarity of song. Later we watched the moon rise over the trees. We felt beauty; we heard and saw it. We tried to clothe the experience with the right words, so we could remember. Well-chosen words need only be few in number, but they help store away the pleasure of the adventure.

We have awakened a small boy at midnight to marvel at the colors in the northern lights. We have stood on hillsides and described the numerous shades of springtime greens across the landscape. It's a marvelous game of awareness and words.

It's a game that can be played anywhere at odd moments. *How do you think a barn in Nebraska looks?* One child may answer, "Red, with cows around it." Another may say, "Gray and lonely, with no trees near." A third older child may become poetic and say, "The barn looks gray and weathered, like it was tired from the summer's heat and weary from icy winter winds."

Each answer is a good one. Yet those who saw less will be pleased by the contributions of those who saw more in their minds. They will sense the living substance of a touch of imagination and try to increase their own use of language. You may be thinking at this point, *I handle words so poorly myself. How can I help my children?* This kind of game teaches everyone and binds you to your children as you share what we call "imaginings."

Try other questions: How does a summer night sound? How does a rainy day feel? What does a kindergarten child look like on her way home from school? I have done this in the classroom. Some children's contributions were dull and uninspired, some were hopeful, others had the bright shine of originality. But each child saw the possibility of words. Natural gifts may differ and, like any other game, contributions should never be the only measure of a person's success. This is only one way of animating the mind in creative effort. But it will help train the ear to listen and the heart to feel beauty and emotion as it comes out in stories that the children later read. The benefits work both ways.

Reading aloud with two teenage boys one summer, we discussed together the elements of writing that made the story so special. They went back through the chapter and found phrases that spelled out beauty like this: "I feel like spring after winter, and sun on the leaves, and like trumpets and harps and all the songs I have ever heard!" The words fairly ring with joy! I covet for both of these boys the ability to use language with even a little of the mastery of the author (J. R. R. Tolkien) whose book we were reading.

The Importance of Words

Since words are the way we communicate experiences, truth, and situations, who should know how to use them more creatively than people who are aware of their Creator? The world cries out for imaginative people who can spell out truth in words that communicate meaningfully to people in their human situation.

Charles Morgan speaks of creative art as "that power to be for the moment a flash of communication between God and man." That concept opens up our horizons to a glimpse of God-huge thoughts, of beauty, of substance beyond our cloddish earthiness, of the immensity of all there is to discover. Using words well is an art.

Yet, tragically, we can live our whole lives inhibited and poverty-stricken in human expression and creativity. We forget to notice, to see what is happening around us. We don't ask questions; we fail to listen. We are afraid of what is different, and are uncertain about what is true and good. Truth and excellence have a way of springing up all over the world, and our role as parents is to teach our children how to find and enjoy the good and to reject what is mediocre and unworthy.

Children are the freest and most imaginative of creatures. They love the fun of words and have a spectacular ability to learn. We must respect their eagerness and competence by introducing them to good books. I am frankly excited by the potential of books to build a whole, healthy, spiritually alert child who has the capacity to enjoy all the possibilities of life.

Emily Dickinson has winsomely captured the spirit of this:

> *He ate and drank the precious words,*
> *His spirit grew robust,*
> *He knew no more that he was poor,*
> *Or that his frame was dust.*
> *He danced along the dingy ways*
> *And this bequest of wings*
> *Was but a book. What liberty*
> *A loosened spirit brings!*[2]

What Good Books Do

Good books have genuine spiritual substance, not just intellectual enjoyment. Books help children know what to look for in life. Reading develops the taste buds of the mind as children learn to savor what is seen, heard, and experienced and fit these into some kind of worthwhile framework.

What is unfamiliar becomes close and real in books. What is ridiculous helps children see the humor in their own lives. Sympathetic understanding is a generous byproduct of sharing the emotions of stories and standing in someone else's shoes. Books are no substitute for life, but a keener pleasure comes to life because of books.

When you've walked across a field with an eight-year-old who comments on the "smell of sweet grass in a sunny pasture," then you'll understand what I mean. Or, a child remembers, "Dandelion stems are full of milk, clover heads are loaded with nectar, and the refrigerator is full of ice-cold drinks. Summer is very nice." Then you hear the words you read from *Charlotte's Web* come back to your own daily experience and agree, "Yes, summer is very nice."

This savoring of life is no small thing. The element of wonder is almost lost today with the onslaught of the media and gadgets of our noisy world. To let a child lose it is to make him blind and deaf to the best of life.

Children have marvelous elasticity of mind. Fancy a child who hasn't met a dragon or a unicorn! Imagine a child who doesn't

Books are no substitute for life, but a keener pleasure comes to life because of books.

[2] *The Poems of Emily Dickinson* (New York: T. Y. Crowell, 1964), p. 20.

Facing failures and tragedies with the characters of a story may vicariously give children the experience of courage and loyalty.

speculate about what small creatures live in a hollow tree or rocky crevice! That's the stuff a sense of wonder may feed on, but when the child is older he will respond with the same sensitivity to a lovely sentence from Monica Shannon's *Dobry:* "Snow is the most beautiful silence in the world."

I have never been able to resist the appeal of a child who asks, "Read to me, please?" The warm security of a little person cuddled close, loving the pictures which help tell the story, listening to the rhythm of the words, laughing in all the right places as the policeman stops Boston traffic for the mother duck and her family in Robert McCloskey's *Make Way for Ducklings.* Or the safe, soothing feeling of Margaret Wise Brown's *Goodnight Moon,* or the wonder of Alvin Tresselt's *White Snow, Bright Snow.*

But the pleasure doesn't end with small children who like to sit on your lap. Growing-up children are just as much fun. Reading Laura Ingalls Wilder's books of pioneer adventure on the prairie, our family could feel the warm cabin, smell the freshly baked bread, hear the blizzard raging outside, and experience with Laura the close family feeling of Pa's singing and fiddling by the fireside. The love and gaiety of the Ingalls' home were shared in our home, and we had a quiet confidence in a family's ability to surmount dangers and hardships.

Books *do* impart a sense of security. Children meet others whose backgrounds, religions, and cultural ways are unlike their own. They come to accept the feeling of being different, and fear, which is the result of not understanding, is removed. Geography invades our living rooms as children visit families from other countries, and the world seems quite friendly.

Facing failures and tragedies with the characters of a story may vicariously give children the experience of courage and loyalty. Weeping with some and rejoicing with others—this is the beginning of a compassionate heart.

Courage is transmitted by heroes like *Johnny Tremain* and even the comical Reepicheep in *The Voyage of the Dawn Treader.* Valor does not belong to an exclusive race of supermen. It is within the hearts of those who are committed to truth and honor, the kind of heroes with whom one can identify. Children have loved the biblical Daniel, David, and Joseph for these same reasons and have gained deeper understanding of the relationship of courage to faith.

One of my young friends read *Call It Courage* at least four times the year he was nine. In transition between being a *child* and being a *boy*, he needed a model for his new manhood. This book fed his heart with ideals and integrity in such practical ways that it is difficult to measure its influence. He said, "It made me feel brave and strong!"

Reading Aloud

Every parent who reads with children and every teacher who shares books knows the wistful sigh that accompanies the request for "one more chapter." The teachers I remember best are those who read to us each day from some wonderful book. I remember with special fondness the English teacher in my high school as she sat on the corner of her desk, enchanting us with the music of Sir Walter Scott's *Lady of the Lake:*

> *The stag at eve had drunk its fill,*
> *Where danced the moon on Monan's rill,*
> *And deep his midnight lair had made*
> *In lone Glenartney's hazel shade.*

Later, in other classrooms I knew the delight of taking children into a great adventure with a story—the utter silence of the room, the intent look on the children's faces, and the involuntary sigh that escaped our lips at the conclusion of the episode. We had been together in the presence of good writing, and we felt bound together by the experience.

Books matter to children. It pleases me that when I meet former students unexpectedly they tell me what they are reading. They could pay me no greater compliment; they know I would want to know. Great literature has a way of building people. Books continue to be an influence far beyond my own words to these children.

What I am saying is simply this: As parents we are concerned about building whole people—people who are alive emotionally, spiritually, intellectually. The instruction to *train up a child in the way he should go* has enormous dimensions. It is to teach a child to think, to influence character, to give high ideals, and to encourage integrity. It is to provide largeness of thought, creative thinking, imaginative wondering. How large are your goals for your children? Why have a small world when you can walk with God into the larger place that is his domain?

Young children, fresh uncluttered minds, the world before them—to what treasures will you lead them? With what will you furnish their spirit?

Pooh and Piglet nearly catch a Woozle.

Chapter 2

Milk and Honey

Children have two basic needs, writes Erich Fromm in *The Art of Loving:* they need both *milk* and *honey* from their parents. *Milk* symbolizes the care given to physical needs: brush your teeth, drink your orange juice, eat your vegetables, get enough sleep. *Honey* symbolizes the sweetness of life, that special quality that makes life sing with enjoyment for all it holds. Fromm says, "Most parents are capable of giving milk, but only a minority of giving honey, too." To give honey, one must love honey and have it to give. Good books are rich in honey, and hence the title of this book.

You have only to read books with children to know how they react to this "honey" in their lives. Some parents can almost recite some picture books they have read over and over to their children. What goes on in the mind of that child who looks and looks, who laughs at all the right places, who wants to turn to the next page, and who at the end asks for another story? Reading to a child is like painting on a canvas.

Big people and little people experience a common joy about reading. When I returned a stack of books I had borrowed from a friend, three-year-old Jim welcomed back these familiar books as old friends, so glad to see them, carefully paging through them, his face lighting up with pleasure as he came upon favorites. Finally he found the special one he was looking for, hugged it, and began reciting

Families have to repeatedly make conscious decisions about what is valuable and then choose the best over the mediocre.

phrases, laughing at some pages, earnestly studying others. Even the size and the feel of the book seemed important to him— a prized possession. My heart warmed just watching him.

Books are important to Jim because they are to his parents. He hears his mother and father talk about books at the dinner table, and they take time to read to him. Books are treated with respect and care, Jim will tell you that. He also will tell you that he will soon be a reader "all by myself."

Making Choices

Parents unconsciously teach their children what is valuable by the way they spend their own time. If television is more important to the parents than books, the children will likely choose the same. If television programs gave exceptional content, then perhaps less would be lost. The allurement of the screen is no small thing, but television, for the most part, has betrayed its potential. It is responsible for dumbing-down and coarsening the fabric of our society. It keeps pushing at the edge of questionable humor and behavior, and in many homes is a monster in the living room, all chairs facing the screen awaiting the next available amusement. Families who care about their children need to monitor how much time is spent in an activity that offers so little in return.

More than ever before, families have to repeatedly make conscious decisions about what is valuable and then choose the best over the mediocre. If appreciation of beauty and the gift of articulation are meaningful to you, then I suggest that exposure to great writing is a necessity.

It's sometimes a choice: reading aloud to a child for a half hour, or calling a friend on the phone. Using the television as morning babysitter, or finding a more imaginative way to entertain a child. Life is full of choices, and I find myself impatient with people who cry "lack of time." We make time for what we think is important, and in doing so we teach our children about what things really matter in life.

Whether we are willing to sacrifice personal choices depends on what our long-range goals are for our children and for our family life. These need to be spelled out so we make wise decisions. What do you want to see happen in your children? In your family?

In Richard Peck's acceptance speech for the Newbery Medal for *A Year Down Yonder*, he tells of his mother reading bedtime stories (because there was *bedtime*—something missing for many children). He says, "I heard my first stories in my mother's voice. A satisfactory substitute for that technique has yet to be devised, because most of who we are is decided in those first five fleeting years of life before we ever see a school."

He continued with this warning statement: "Powerful forces divorce the young from their roots and traditions: the relentlessness of the video game that is the pornography of the prepubescent, a violent virtual reality that eliminates the parents who paid for it. And the peer group that rushes in to fill the vacuum of the teacher's vanished authority and an awesome parental power failure." Those are strong words, but for many families these are true words.

We don't really need to be pushed around by the press of life; we just think we do. Somehow we have given value to being overly committed. In most cases, we have freedom and capacity to choose. Cultural pressures are real; make no mistake about that. But who wants the culture to run their lives? Each set of parents is charged with responsibility for their children. They must *choose* goals they consider valuable and then make private decisions to implement them. Life is full of choices between good, better, and best. Only lazy parents avoid making decisions. And remember, parents are the ones who bend the twig.

The plea I am making is simply this—make time for books! Don't let your children live in spiritual poverty when abundance is available! Fill your children up with words, with imaginative worlds, with adventures beyond your ken.

What Kinds of Books?

What kind of books are proper fare for a child's mind? Discovering these will lift your own heart and give you a taste for honey. Once you begin enjoying good children's literature, you will find yourself in a treasure house of reading. In your eagerness over discovering children's literature, you need to be careful not to push your children into books beyond their years. It could mean missing those books tailored for their present age.

What kind of books? "Stories that make for wonder. Stories that make for laughter. Stories that stir one within with an understanding of the true nature of courage, of love, of beauty. Stories that make one tingle with high adventure, with daring, with grim determination, with the capacity of seeing danger through to the end.

Snow is to roll in

Buttons are to
keep people warm

From *A Hole Is to Dig* by Ruth Krauss, illustrated by Maurice
Sendak. Copyright © 1952, as to text, by Ruth Krauss.
Copyright © 1952, as to pictures, by Maurice Sendak.
Reprinted with permission of Harper & Row, Publishers.

A good book is always an experience containing spiritual, emotional, and intellectual dimensions.

Stories that bring our minds to kneel in reverence; stories that show the tenderness of true mercy, the strength of loyalty, the unmawkish respect for what is good."[1] These wonderfully descriptive words from Ruth Sawyer in excite me as a book lover. A good book is always an experience containing spiritual, emotional, and intellectual dimensions.

Picture books are a child's first introduction to the world of reading. A child *reads* pictures, expecting the pictures to tell the story and to tell it accurately. Who can know all the impressions and data children store up in their private world from picture books? Such books provide the fun of looking, but they also give an experience. By sharing their own observations, parents teach their children how to look at pictures.

Some concept of art values will begin to form in the child's mind as he looks at pictures. The illustrations in a book are a prime part of the story. Choose books that contain good illustrations; too many cutesy Walt Disney versions can stunt anyone's art appreciation. Exposing children to a variety of art helps them choose what they like. Make a point of commenting on colors and artistic expression. The book listing in the later chapters designates outstanding illustrators.

However, remember that you are dealing with children. Your view of art may not always be a child's view of pleasing art. I'm thinking particularly of some of the artwork done by illustrator Maurice Sendak, a favorite with children. Something of the child in me responds to his hilarious drawings. But librarians gasped in horror when *Where the Wild Things Are* was chosen as a Caldecott Medal winner. One children's librarian told me she was appalled, feeling certain children would reject it. To her surprise there was a raid on every copy in the library.

Why did the children like it so much? Because Sendak pictured what they would have drawn in the story of rebellious Max and his adventure with the Wild Things. Mr. Sendak was deluged with drawings sent to him by children, their own creations of Wild Things.

A book can have surprising effects. An apathetic, unresponsive four-year-old in a day-care center in Brooklyn could not be coaxed to speak except for an occasional indistinct utterance. Slow improvement began to appear in the storytelling time, and when the teacher chose *Where the Wild Things Are*, the child listened and looked intently. Afterward she approached the teacher and uttered her first sentence, "May I have that book?" Something in that book opened up

[1]Ruth Sawyer, *The Way of a Storyteller* (New York: Viking Press, 1962), p. 157.

a needy little girl, who has since become an avid lover of books and an affectionate child.

Many times children say, "Now I'll read you this story," and then proceed to read what the pictures are saying. Or, sometimes a child says, "Don't read the writing, read the pictures." Begin to notice illustrators you and your children like and look for their work. (Incidentally, some artists change their style over a period of time. Mr. Sendak's later illustrations are not nearly as happy and light as his earlier ones in *A Hole Is to Dig* or even his *Wild Things* drawings.)

Choosing Good Stories

Quality is a high priority. Good stories have good writing. They use imagery and word pictures that inspire the imagination. C. S. Lewis's children's books stand in a class apart for excellence. The Narnia Chronicles are worth reading over and over by every child and in every family. They are profoundly good books on every level—theme, plot, characters, action, language. That places the standard high, but there are more books than can be mentioned that qualify as excellent—which is the point of the book list in this book.

It is better to acquaint your child with a book of quality than with second-rate writing where the plot is only a thin disguise for dumping a message. Children have a precocious skill for skipping paragraphs, pages, and whole chapters if they feel a sermon coming, says Paul Hazard in his classic work on children's books.[2]

Every family should own one good Bible storybook so that children become familiar with the wonderful stories of the Old Testament and meet Jesus in the New Testament. It is important to acquaint children with literature and stories that are foundational to our whole culture. If God is important to you, this will become a vital part of your sharing with your children. But that's only the beginning. There is a whole world of wonder awaiting a child in books.

On our bookshelves stand twenty-three small volumes of the works of Beatrix Potter, sized to fit little hands. The copyright dates are in the early 1900s, but I expect them to be as popular with our great-grandchildren as with our children. Her picture stories should be among the first for a child's personal library. Her illustrations are timeless, an inseparable part of her stories; her characterizations are brief, but ever so lucid. Your children simply must meet Peter Rabbit, Johnny Town Mouse, Squirrel Nutkin, Jemima Puddle Duck, Jeremy Fisher, and other unforgettable characters.

[2]Paul Hazard, *Books, Children and Men* (Boston, Mass.: Horn Books, 1960).

It was from Miss Potter that I first learned how much children love big words. Miss Potter's economy of words—she chooses just the right one while other authors might require many—gives liveliness to her stories, but every so often she tucks in a gem of a new word for children to roll over their tongues. The sparrows in *The Tale of Peter Rabbit* "implore him to exert himself" when Peter is caught in a net by his jacket buttons. The gentleman fox in *The Tale of Jemima Puddle Duck* is "hospitable" and speaks of Jemima "commencing her tedious setting on the eggs," and Jemima herself complains of a "superfluous" hen who is too lazy to do so.

Does this turn children off? No, seemingly not. I gathered my conclusions when I heard our own small child *implore* one of his friends to *exert himself.* Dr. Seuss makes the most of a child's fascination with words in his books, devising words out of his imagination that delight children, regardless of what adults think of them. Could it be that all words belong to children as much as to adults?

From *The Tale of Peter Rabbit* by Beatrix Potter, copyright © Frederick Warne & Co., Ltd. Used by permission.

Families can grow together by discovering the fun of words. Happy is the home that has one parent at least who says, "Let's look it up!" and helps children to see that a dictionary is a fascinating friend. I remember the day *ubiquitous* occurred in something we read aloud together and with what pride that word became part of our household vocabulary. We used it *ubiquitously.*

What about Fairy Tales?

Some parents are troubled by fairy tales. I heard a father say that life wasn't really like *Cinderella* and that wicked stepmothers who want to kill beautiful daughters aren't the best fare for a child's mind. Others don't like elves and fairies and talking animals. Some refuse even Santa Claus.

You'll have to make up your own mind, but I, for one, like *Cinderella* and elves and talking animals and even Santa Claus. Children don't take life as seriously as adults and are more inclined to read for pleasure without theorizing until all the fun is wrung out. I laughed over a story told by a mother, who suspected that her son had discovered that tooth fairies and Santa Claus were make-believe. He told her, "I have discovered that Santa Claus, the Easter Bunny, and the tooth fairy all have one thing in common." She waited to hear his discovery. He said, "They are all nocturnal."

Fairy tales don't condone poor behavior; they simply relate what occurs. Children learn very early that there are good people, bad people, kind people, cruel people, and assortments of behavior in between. And children have room in their lives for all sorts of miracles.

That's the problem, someone will say. If you let them believe in fairies and fantasy, how will they distinguish between truth and falsehood? I can't help thinking that since children love make-believe, they can easily tell the difference. At our house we have wondered if the silvery, dewy spiderwebs sparkling in the early morning sun had been part of the decorations for a ball the fairies held the night before, especially if orange toadstools have sprung up in the same area. We discussed it as if it were true, but it was like sharing a special secret. We all knew it was make-believe. There is nothing unspiritual about an active imagination, a token of the liberty of childhood.

One of my young friends, at three, told me about the tiger who lived in her backyard. I inquired about where she kept him and what she fed him, and she told me the details with great delight. Then I told her about the tiger who lived in *my* backyard. Her eyes danced as I described his strange behavior and that he had purple stripes. Then she came very close and whispered, "Is yours a real one?" When I said it wasn't, she said confidentially, "Mine isn't either."

Was I encouraging her to lie? I think not. Both of us were in on the world of pretend—a legitimate adventure. How quickly we want to quench the fine spirit of childhood. Imagination is the stuff out of which creativity comes, and this little girl's artwork already shows a skillful amount of this rare ingredient.

Our ten-year-old got into an earnest discussion with a group of young adults, one of whom was stating positively that when he had children he would never tell them about Santa Claus because when they found out he wasn't real maybe the children wouldn't believe him about things that were true, like God, for example. After listening to the debate, our son came up with his contribution. "I knew about Santa Claus, like I knew about elves and other pretend things. I never got him mixed up with God because I could tell from the way my parents talked and acted what was true."

If your experience has been different, perhaps we should only conclude that there are a number of variables of personality, emphasis, and

*Some nonsense is
good for everyone.*

other intangibles that might make it so. C. S. Lewis once commented "that we who still enjoy fairy tales have less reason to wish actual childhood back. We have kept its pleasures and added some grownup ones as well."

A. A. Milne's *Winnie-the-Pooh* and *The House at Pooh Corner* are examples of some of the finest kind of make-believe—the ageless kind. One small child asked, "Are you reading a children's book or am I reading a grown-up book?" because that's the way *Winnie-the-Pooh* is. It's full of talking animals with lovable personalities and exceedingly humorous situations, for which age only increases appreciation.

Which brings us to the subject of humorous stories; a child's reading should be sprinkled with them. From the ludicrous situation of *Horton Hatches an Egg* to the more subtle humor and wisdom of *The Wind in the Willows* to the simpler boyish adventures of *Homer Price* and *Henry Huggins* or the magical girl named *Pippi Longstocking* who lives with a horse and a monkey—give your child large doses of these. Some nonsense is good for everyone, like the unforgettable tea party in *Alice in Wonderland*.

As children grow older they will enjoy tales of courage (*Call It Courage, The Matchlock Gun*), stories about animals (*King of the Wind, Sounder, The Yearling*), adventure stories (*Caddie Woodlawn, My Side of the Mountain*), and a wealth of experience in mysteries. Biographies, epic hero tales, and historical novels are all part of rounding out the reading picture.

Some children like how-to-do-it or all-about-everything type books, but I suspect parents like them best because they look so educational. These really should be in a separate category because they don't usually classify as literature but are more nearly manuals of information. Paul Hazard suggests that instead of pouring out so much knowledge on a child's soul that it is crushed, we should plant a seed of an idea that will develop from inside. The most important knowledge is of the human heart, he concludes.

What about Classic Books?

Parents, hearing about classics, are sometimes conditioned against them because they feel that surely dullness and classic must go together. Sometimes this is because books we call classics are introduced poorly or too early. I prefer to call them "good books." They are classics because they have demonstrated the enduring qualities of good literature (discussed in chapter 3). We must read them as they were written, even though some publishers may diminish or simplify the story for popular reading. To do that is to end up with only a story, because the *classic* elements have either been deleted or diluted.

Many of the stories listed in my book list have been around for more than sixty years, some for over a hundred. They are being read because readers still love them. The characters are memorable and stay in the hearts of children now grown into parents who want their children to know these same wonderful characters.

One such book is Kate Douglas Wiggin's *Rebecca of Sunnybrook Farm*, first published in 1903. After reading it in 1904, Jack London, author of *The Call of the Wild*, wrote to Ms. Wiggin from the headquarters of the First Japanese Army in Manchuria. "May I thank you for *Rebecca?*" he wrote. "I would have quested the wide world over to make her mine, only I was born too long ago, and she was born but yesterday. Why could she not have been my daughter? Why couldn't it have been I who bought the three hundred cakes of soap? Why, O why?"

That same irrepressible, ten-year-old *Rebecca* is still in print and still inspiring admiration. Which only tells you what a classic book can do. Look for books labeled "well-loved" or "classic"—and enjoy them yourself. (One of the great things about being a parent is that you get to catch up on all the books you missed in your own childhood!)

Should We Censor Some Books?

The word *censor* carries the connotation of supervising the morality of other people. That is a heavy task. I suggest we "choose" instead of censor. Censors usually get into trouble because they take their own standards and insist that others abide by them. While there are things we want to censor for the good of society (i.e., pornography), such things are usually clearly noted as destructive by society as a whole. Apart from clear guidance, we usually need a good dose of humility when we think of censoring someone else's choices.

We also need wisdom to choose rightly ourselves. Life is full of choosing one thing and rejecting another. We must even decide between good, better, and best. We choose some books and reject others—and for different reasons. Some books are a waste of time; others are profane or too explicit in detail. We choose some as being well-written and others as being poorly written; some we disapprove of because of unworthy subject matter, while we choose others *because of* their subject matter. We choose for ourselves (and our families) but not for others.

Seldom does the subject of censoring children's books arise, but the popular and controversial Harry Potter books recently have been under fire. The controversy was heightened by an article on www.theonion.com, a website that specializes in spoof news stories and humor. (In one story a 350-pound woman sues Hershey's chocolate company.) *The Onion* put out a spoof release on the Internet telling how children were practicing witchcraft as a result of reading about Harry Potter, a boy who attends a school for wizards. The spoof somehow ended up as an email that some people took seriously. These people added fuel to the fire and sent it to an even wider circle of friends. The end result was an uproar that only increased the sales of the book. Most of the people who registered complaints at school board meetings or to librarians had never read the books. Rule #1: Don't criticize what you haven't read yourself. A kind of mob psychology demands censorship. Fear tends to take away sound thinking.

During those months of furor I spent a good amount of time defending a kid who goes to Hogwarts School for Wizards, something I had never done before. While it is true that we don't want to encourage children to explore witchcraft or engage in casting spells, these books do not promote any such actions. J. K. Rowling has created a series of books about a parallel world, using imaginative devices (owls that deliver mail; portraits that guard doors; Quidditch, a fascinating game played on a flying broomstick; a school motto, *Never tickle a sleeping dragon*), a fast-moving plotline, and likable protagonists. The books satisfy the love of mystery and magic in everyone. This is fantasy. Bravery, courage, loyalty, humility, and the fight

Ten Ways to Raise a Nonreader

1. Have the television on at all times. Make sure you put a television set and a computer in every room. (Don't forget the kitchen!)
2. Keep the place neat—no books or literary magazines in sight.
3. Never let your children see you read a book.
4. Never take your kids to the library.
5. Never read stories aloud past age two.
6. Never talk about ideas while eating meals.
7. Keep the lights down low. Buy only forty-watt lightbulbs.
8. Schedule your children for every activity you can think of so they won't be bored.
9. Never play any table games together.
10. Absolutely no reading in bed or good lamps to make it easy to do.

between good and evil are themes in these books.

What about the witchcraft element? I suggest parents read books 1–3 with their children and talk about the stories. It is a good opportunity to talk about witchcraft and what the Bible says about it. Read Deuteronomy 18:9–12 and ask your children why God forbids the practice of sorcery. Disarm any potential danger of the stories by talking about them. And then have fun reading them together.[2]

My favorite illustration about this situation came from librarian Kimbra Wilder Gish, who recounted the story of Sleeping Beauty. Remember the witch at Beauty's birth predicted that she would prick her finger on a spindle when she was sixteen and fall asleep forever. Her frightened parents banned every spindle in the kingdom, or so they thought. On Beauty's sixteenth birthday she wandered into the attic room of the tower, saw an unfamiliar spindle, and curiosity caused her to prick her finger and thus fulfill the witch's prophecy. How much better it would have been if the king and queen had warned Beauty about the potential danger of spindles in her life and thus avoided her tragedy!

As parents you have the right not to read to your children any book that troubles you. (I found myself reading the Disney version of Bambi one day to a small son who wept bitterly, refusing to be consoled. I would not choose that book again.) But when we do not choose a book we make that decision for *ourselves*, not for another family, a school, or the population in general. As for the Harry Potter books, I have only read the first four at this writing.

Ten Ways to Raise a Reader

1. Restrict television watching drastically.
2. Keep the computer under control and where it can be monitored. Don't allow too many hours on pointless computer games or in chat rooms.
3. Have books and other good reading material within easy reach, an enticement to read.
4. Let your children see you reading.
5. Read books aloud together regardless of age.
6. Talk about books together; play games together.
7. Have well-lit rooms with comfortable chairs that invite reading.
8. Balance activity schedules with reading time. Let your kids know the library is as important as the gymnasium.
9. Encourage reading in bed with good lights to do so.
10. Visit the library often, and listen to books-on-tape when traveling.

---

[2]Don't blame Harry Potter books for what some businesses are doing to exploit the idea of witches and spells, producing companion products that promote many ideas not in the books.

Children latch on to wonder more quickly than error.

So far I do not see the stories promoting eastern religion, New Age, or whatever—not even true witchcraft. Two books will give you more thinking about the pros and cons of this issue: Connie Neal's *What's a Christian to Do with Harry Potter?* (pro) and Richard Abanes's *Harry Potter and the Bible* (con). Both are done by thoughtful people.

In any event, comparing the Harry Potter books to the Narnia Chronicles by C. S. Lewis or J. R. R. Tolkien's trilogy is not helpful. The moral complexity of evil and goodness in the fantasies of Lewis and Tolkien is profoundly biblical and engages readers on a far deeper level. In that sense there is no comparison. The fact that all three authors refer to wizards and witches is not a relevant issue. This is fantasy literature. J. K. Rowling also places Harry Potter in a world with moral order: choices have consequences, good and evil are at stake, and practical wisdom spills out of the believable tensions of his life, but it is on a different level and has a different significance. Rowling is a good storyteller, and her characters find themselves in situations that reveal "truths," if you will, that give readers much to think about and talk about together. That the Harry Potter books, like many other stories, are not constructed within a specifically Christian worldview can be noted without detracting from the helpful insights and fun found in these books. It's part of understanding literature. We do the Harry Potter books an injustice when we assign meanings that are not in the stories.

Get on with Reading

Personally, I'd rather get on with reading rather than censoring. Most ideas that create fear and distrust are defused by talking about the ideas. Children latch on to wonder more quickly than error. It's the grown-ups who fail to see the wonder and stumble over what children think are trivial concerns. A world of wonder and books awaits us.

What kind of books? "Stories that make for wonder. Stories that make for laughter. Stories that stir one within with an understanding of the true nature of courage, of love, of beauty. Stories that make one tingle with high adventure, with daring, with grim determination, with the capacity of seeing danger through to the end. Stories that bring our minds to kneel in reverence; stories that show the tenderness of true mercy, the strength of loyalty, the unmawkish respect for what is good."

Honey is a special treat, not a medicinal treatment.

In James Stephen's *The Crock of Gold*, a wise philosopher says, "I have learned that the head does not hear anything until the heart has listened, and what the heart knows today the head will understand tomorrow." What a reservoir of wisdom good literature can store away for the heart!

Happy, happy it is to be
Where the greenwood hangs o'er the dark blue sea;
To roam in the moonbeams clear and still
And dance with the elves
Over dale and hill;
To taste their cups, and with them roam
The fields for dewdrops and honeycomb.

WALTER DE LA MARE, "ANN AND THE FAIRY SONG"

Chapter 3

What Makes a Good Book?

C.S. Lewis said that no book is really worth reading at the age of ten which is not equally worth reading at the age of fifty. Children's books cannot be written *for* or down *to* children. Children reject books that do not treat them as equals. The "My dear little reader" approach never really pleased children. Books are written not so much *for* children as written *by* people who have not lost their childhood. Since adults are really only grown-up children, good books appeal to all ages.

Kids and Books

It's hard to imagine a time when "books" were found only in synagogues, churches, or other public places because they were too rare for ordinary people to own. When the printing press was first invented, no one could project to a day when there would be libraries full of books for children. When books became more common, adults foisted only dull, moralistic books on children. Adults were surprised by the way children in the early 1700s appropriated Daniel Defoe's *Robinson Crusoe* for their very own, a tale of adventure if ever there was one. Hans Christian Andersen was unique in his contribution to children and his capacity for being a grown-up child. In many ways he turned the tide in children's literature by the mid–1800s.

*A good book has
a profound kind
of morality*

The development of children's literature is surely one of the most enriching and life-enhancing achievements I can think of. Now we have libraries and bookstores full of the most creative literature for children the world has ever seen—and yet, instead of reveling in this gift, many people take it for granted and even ignore reading as a valuable way to spend time. The athletic fields surrounding our schools demonstrate where most families spend their time and energy. That's not to denigrate the value of athletics; it is simply a plea for balance so that the heartbeat of school life is not only the gymnasium, but the library as well.

Good books have a life force that propels children forward. Books release something creative in the minds of those who absorb them. The author captures reality, the permanent stuff of life, and something is aroused in the heart of the reader that endures. Sometimes the author reveals the ridiculous and makes us laugh, but always a good book is imaginative and leaves something rich behind in the reader's mind.

Childhood is so brief and yet so open and formative that we must not neglect our responsibility to furnish it with what we know is good. Impressions are taken into maturity; we are shaping a future. I cannot believe that children exposed to the best of literature will later choose that which is cheap and demeaning. That is why only the rarest kind of best is good enough for children.

Good books are about the stuff that makes up life. Most books are about relationships—sibling and friends, parents and children—and the emotions these relationships engender—joy and sorrow, hate and love, admiration and envy, anger and hope. This is essentially true of fiction and nonfiction and even fantasy. Every child needs to see the possibilities of being human, watch the consequence of choices, and have their hearts stretched by goodness and courage in action.

A good book has a profound kind of morality—not a cheap, sentimental sort that thrives on shallow plots and superficial heroes, but the sort of force that inspires the reader's inner life and draws out what is noble. A good writer has something worthy to say and says it in the best possible way. The author respects the child's ability to understand. Principles are not preached; they are implicit in the plotting of the story.

Classics Keep Coming Back

The bond between a child and a book can be everlasting. Parents need to think long and hard about giving away favorite children's books when they think "they are past that age." One has only to hear the despair in a parent's voice when they hear that a favorite book from their childhood is no longer in print. Some of these books have become collector's items for this reason.

In the last seventy-five years, the writing of children's books has flourished. Many of the books published fifty years ago or more are still in print and have taken on the stature of classics. Listing children's books is an enduring proposition when these are chosen.

We sigh with sadness when something goes out of print. Then, because of the quality of the book, it turns up again in a new edition on the bookshelves. What a wonderful boon for a generation of parents looking for books they loved as children!

One of the happiest of these new editions are the Little Tim books by Edward Ardizzone, just-right stories for adventure-loving six-year-olds. The first book, *Little Tim and the Brave Sea Captain*, introduces Tim, a boy who lives by the sea and "wanted very much to be a sailor." Subsequent books record Tim's incredible seafaring adventures and are peopled with memorable characters. Roger Duvoisin's *Petunia* has made an overdue comeback as a fiftieth anniversary edition. Petunia is an addlebrained goose who finds a book which she carries around under her wing, thinking its presence will make her wise enough to give advice to other farmyard creatures. Eventually, a chastened Petunia learns that "it is not enough to carry wisdom under my wing." The six original Babar books written and illustrated by Jean de Brunhoff are back in print in a gift edition, *Bonjour, Babar!* de Brunoff is considered the father of the picture book. And there are others.

While comeback editions of fiction for older readers are not as plentiful, Joan Aiken's Wolves Chronicles have been rescued from oblivion. These are a series of "historical" novels set in England during the reign of King James III, a time she invented herself. Of the series only *The Wolves of Willoughby Chase* has remained in print. Now others like *Nightbirds on Nantucket, Black Hearts of Battersea, The Cuckoo Tree,* and *The Stolen Lake* have attractive new editions.

Those who loved the Betsy-Tacy series by Maud Hart Lovelace will be glad to see these reissued, even though they may miss the original covers of these wonderful stories about little girls growing up in Minnesota in the early 1900s. Other golden-oldies have new gift editions, with Willy Pogany's 1928 *Mother Goose* being one of the most unusual. Thanks, publishers, for continuing to nourish us with good books.

Read the Original Version

In almost every instance, the book as originally written is the best. Simplifying great writing means less-than-great writing. If you want to read *Bambi*, then read it as Felix Salten wrote it, not the sentimentalized popular Disney version. Julie Andrews as *Mary Poppins* has a charm of its own, but that Mary Poppins is not the character Pamela Travers wrote about. If you would know Winnie-the-Pooh and his friends, it is best to meet them in A. A. Milne's original prose, with Ernest Shepard's drawings. Don't buy diluted editions.

The bookshelves in many homes hold only Disney versions of classics, Sesame Street stories, Barney tales, or whatever is currently on television and in children's films. For most children their only acquaintance with the classics comes from Disney, whose books are produced to help market their movies and which often bear little likeness to the original. Since fairy tales are in public domain, they are literally eviscerated for the purposes of the filmmaker.

Kari Jensen Gold, a New York columnist, highlights one of the most offensive examples of this that occurs in *The Little Mermaid*. Hans Christian Andersen's original story of *The Little Mermaid* (translated by Neil Philip) begins like this:

> Far out to sea the water is blue as the petals of the loveliest cornflower and as clear as the purest glass; but is deep, deeper than any anchor can reach. Countless church steeples would have to be piled one on top of the other to stretch from the sea bed to the surface. That's where the sea folk live.

That's the way a fairy tale ought to begin. Think of what a child can see and feel as this is read. The cadence of the words is like a song and sets the mood for the story.

In contrast, the Disney version begins like this (it almost pains me to record it!):

> Ariel was sixteen, the age when a mermaid was supposed to be thinking about marrying a merboy and settling down. But Ariel had other things on her mind.

From the start this becomes a different story, not the classic. First, the mermaid is named. Could there be some reason why Hans Christian Andersen did not name her? Was it an oversight or was it because

*"Mary Poppins," they cried.
"Mary Poppins, come back!"*

Illustration by Mary Shepard.
Reproduced from *Mary Poppins Comes Back,* copyright © 1935, 1962
by P. L. Travers by permission of Harcourt, Brace Jovanovich, Inc.

it is more mysterious not to be named, and that nameless she would have a universal appeal, and could maybe even be me?

The hints are in the Disney version. Politically correct Ariel is not going to settle down with a merboy (whatever that is!). She has bigger plans than that. The little mermaid seems a desperate girl looking for affection. She shows none of the sensitivity to life issues and the world outside the sea that is found in the original. The stakes have changed dramatically. All Ariel needs is a kiss from Prince Eric!

In Andersen's tale the mermaid is described: "She was a strange child, quiet and thoughtful." At stake is something far different. This mermaid, seeking to know what lies above the sea, comes to understand who she is, to know sacrifice and love, choice and sorrow, redemption and truth. Check that out against the ending of the Disney version. The contrast sets the teeth on edge.

Yet for all of this, my biggest objection is raising children on stories in which the language is so uninspired and trite. The loss of words put together in the right way cheats the reader. Popularized versions often become trivial stories with bad prose. If you want children to speak and write good language, then they need to hear beautiful language in their stories. If you want them to know memorable characters, then read the original story, rather than a popularized version.

One of my friends commented that her children's schoolrooms seem to have few classics available. More books are chosen as teaching aids for social studies than for their lasting influence on children. If children are going to hear the good and the beautiful, parents need to be certain to serve such fare at home.

Included in my bibliography are only two simplified versions. One is *Little Pilgrim's Progress* for younger children or one of the several fine condensed and modernized versions now available for older children and adults. Neither of these approximates the depth of writing of John Bunyan's original manuscript, which is probably more readable than the King James Bible. The marvelous imagery of this great book is couched in Bunyan's excellent prose. If you are among the families who choose the original, you will then have read Bunyan. But I am a realist. To miss any experience at all of the spiritual exercise and imagery of *Pilgrim's Progress* seems too great a loss to me, so I have included the simplified versions. The literary heart of the book may sometimes be missing, but the ideas still are of epic proportions. Your children will be caught up in the wonder of Christian's journey and be exposed to great truths.

The second simplification is the well-done *Tales from Shakespeare*, which hopefully will prepare the reader to enjoy Shakespeare at a later date. Charles Lamb and his sister Mary wrote these condensations of the plots of Shakespeare's plays in the early 1800s; that they are still in print says something about their excellence.

The film version of any story is seldom as good as the book. Tom Sawyer must be met in a book, no matter how well the television version is received. I cajoled our son into reading Twain, and he had no embarrassment in thanking me. He commented, "What the words help you to see and feel inside is much better than television!" That is true of almost every book. Don't let a "cute" video of Pooh keep you from meeting the real Pooh in a book!

The problem with television, movies, and videos is that they kill personal creativity. We don't need an imagination to wonder what the characters look like. While a good actor can portray intense emotion, what the language of the story brings to the reader is a far different experience. Films can cheat us of the opportunity to learn how to express what we feel in words. Reading is the direct opposite of television. No wonder writer Julius Lester said, "The failure of modern living is the failure of the imagination. . . . Literature is the royal road that enables us to enter the realm of the imagination."

Reinventing Old Books

L. Frank Baum wrote *The Wizard of Oz* back in 1900. He produced nearly a book a year in the Oz series until his death in 1919. Publishers, seeing a marketing opportunity, hired hack writers to continue writing the Oz series until forty volumes completed the series! No wonder librarians looked askance at the Wizard when they saw how much shelf space he was taking. If Baum's writing and imagination sparked the success of the books, what do you think happened when hack writers began turning out sequels?

Series books have always run the risk of losing their steam if the series continues too long even with the original author. But now publishers are once again looking at popular books as a "brand" and are creating "brand-extenders." In some cases they commission other authors or artists to take a well-known series and continue the stories after the original creator's death. The stories then no longer bear the creativity that attracted us in the first place, only the familiar character.

The Laura Ingalls Wilder stories have been rewritten and made into beginner chapter books, "Little House Chapter Books." These slender volumes give speedy, upbeat, bare-bones treatment to the colorful and creative descriptions and events in the original books. By eliminating all potentially challenging elements, like the description of the beautiful dress Ma wore to the party (read about it in *Little House in the Big Woods*), the stories also eliminate the aura around Ma that made her so elegant, so that she "looked so rich and fine that Laura was afraid to touch her."

Commenting on this in an article in *Horn Book* magazine called "Little House on the Bottom Line," Christine Hepperman laments the way the chapter books eliminate pioneer realities such as Pa's hunting that kept the family in food, significantly changing the story line to favor animal-rights thinking. While the charm of The Little House books is their accurate depiction of scenes like those from *By the Shores of Silver Lake* where Laura and her sister find scraps of old calico and in secret construct Christmas gifts, now there are Little House picture books, calendars, sticker books, craft books—all with commercial success in mind and less opportunity for creativity on the part of the reader. The saddest part is that these stories are being trivialized before children reach the reading level required by the original. We can only hope they do not succeed in doing this with the Chronicles of Narnia.

Again, if you stick with the original version, you have what the author wanted to give you, and that is usually a winner.

What Makes One Book Superior and Another Inferior?

Let's begin by taking apart the elements of a book. First, we begin with the idea behind the book. What is the author trying to say? We call this the *theme*, and a weak theme results in a flabby story. It's always good to ask the question, What is this story saying? What is its point?

To get across the theme, the writer must use words, language. How the author uses language is called *style*. Every writer forms his sentences differently and thus weaves his personality into his writing. Word choices reveal the author's skill because they carry action, emotion, truth—and make the music of good prose.

The *plot* of a story is the design given to the idea of the story. Good plots grow out of strong themes. Plot doesn't answer "What happened next?" Plot answers "Why?" The plot holds the story together in such a way that events take on meaning. Involved in plot is *characterization*. The skill with which the author makes the characters memorable and makes them live for us determines in large measure the quality of the story.

What a difference between the characters of Robert Louis Stevenson's *Treasure Island* and a story where the characters are like puppets on a string, enabling the reader to outguess the author. Who can forget Long John Silver, the pirate of pirates? Terrifying, yet somehow likable; cruel, yet somehow kind; he is no stereotyped, one-handed character. If Stevenson had less artistry in defining his characters and plot, a wildly unrealistic piece of writing would have resulted, and we would have long since forgotten Long John Silver.

What a convincing person Mary Poppins is! How unforgettable is Frodo of the Hobbit books or Toad of Toad Hall. Children can't define what charms them, but give them the right thing and they recognize it. They will have little use for stories that are shallow, insipid, awkward, labored, and overly moralistic.

Letters come regularly to the publisher addressed to Laura Ingalls Wilder, author of the Little House on the Prairie series. Long since dead, Laura is still alive to these children. One child wrote, "Oh, Laura, if I was you I would have kicked Nellie Oleson in the leg when she was mean to you!"

Another mother told a children's book editor that when they moved to a more spacious apartment with a guest room, her son had asked eagerly, "Now can Mr. White come and stay overnight with us?" At first she didn't know who he was talking about, but then remembered that this little boy loved E. B. White's stories; *Charlotte's Web* was his favorite. He knew Mr. White as his friend and wanted a visit.

When C. S. Lewis was still living, a ten-year-old we know sent one of her stories to him for his critique and asked him about his method for plotting stories. She wanted to know if he figured out ahead of time how his characters should act. Because he was C. S. Lewis, he answered her as seriously as he would have answered a letter from another professor. In his pinched tiny handwriting, he

Wilbur blushed, "But I'm not terrific, Charlotte. I'm just average for a pig."

From *Charlotte's Web* by E. B. White, illustrated by Garth Williams. Reprinted with permission of Harper & Row, Publishers.

A sense of permanent worthwhileness surrounds really great literature.

wrote back to tell her that his characters often did things that surprised him, that he sometimes couldn't seem to control them. She could understand that because hers did, too. Children do know.

The quality of the idea, the skill of the plot, the depth of the characterization, the distinctive style of the author—that's the best I can do by way of defining a good book. When you find one, you recognize it.

No one has yet sat down and devised a set of rules that magically produces a great story. The quality that we have talked about has to come from the quality inside the person writing the story. In 1945 Jesse Jackson wrote *Call Me Charley*, the story of the only black boy in a white school. Mr. Jackson did not write primarily to deliver a message on race relations. He simply wrote a book out of his own experience. It had the ring of reality, and twenty years later the book's editor would hear a woman tell how she had read a book in the fifth grade that changed her life, her whole attitude about people. The book was *Call Me Charley*.

That which is excellent has a certain spirit of literature present. The sensitivity of the reader says, "This is true." "This is real." And it sets in action something in the reader that has profound effects. It has been an experience—spiritual, imaginative, intellectual, or social. A sense of permanent worthwhileness surrounds really great literature. Laughter, pain, hunger, satisfaction, love, and joy—the ingredients of human life are found in depth and leave a residue of mental and spiritual richness in the reader.

If we familiarize our children with this kind of writing, then they have a ground for making comparisons. Not everything they read will be excellent, but they will know a story's possibilities. It will set their reading patterns in motion.

Take Time to Explore Books

Clearly we are living in a time of richness in children's literature. We have almost too much to choose from, which makes visits to the library and bookstore confusing. Where does one begin?

I have already mentioned the importance of illustrations. A great variety of styles should be part of a child's inheritance, not just the parent's current preference. Bright colors, gentle pastels, bold strokes, whimsical lines, quaint old-fashioned pictures, modern design, pen and ink sketches—the story will demand a certain mood for the child. As time goes on your family will have its favorite illustrators.

Some books simply look more readable than others. White space, style of type, and paper quality may draw you to a book. That is to say, a good book should look like a good book! I respond warmly to the lovely borders on each page of the Jan Brett books, like *The Mitten*, borders that encourage you to peek at the next page.

We hardly praise the quality of what is available today because that's all we know. It wasn't always that way. I found *A Child's History of England* by Charles Dickens in the bottom of a box when cleaning out a friend's house. The book cover read "Profusely Illustrated." Every fourth page had an excellent black and white drawing, only a few showing much action. Most were portraits of kings, queens, and other famous people—certainly not pictures to capture a child's imagination. Charles Dickens' prose is excellent, but I doubt any child today would finish it because its pages are crowded with tiny print and its format does not draw the reader into the book. This didn't stop children of yesteryear because they had no comparison.

Libraries are intimidating to the uninitiated. So many books, so many shelves—how does one choose? A few children whose parents have taught them which authors to look for or how to choose a book may invade the library with the confidence of a vacuum cleaner, scooping up everything good in sight. But for most this is not true. Parents know what I mean, because without some help, they feel a similar bewilderment. Librarians are there to help. Only a small percentage of parents take advantage of the librarian's skill and ask for help. Take your time. Go to the library often. Knowing about good books requires some learning time.

That's why I have written this book. My book list does not contain *all* the good books available, but it is a beginning. These have stood the test of time and/or of children's choice. Notice authors' names and teach your children to do likewise. It's the secret to conquering library fear. If your older child enjoys one of Kate Seredy's books (and I hope she does!), then she will doubtless want to read others by this author. Experience is the best teacher.

It's better to say, "This looks like fun!" or "Here's one you might enjoy" or "What do you think of this book?" instead of "Here is a book you must read." A child may decide without opening the cover that this is just the book he does *not* want to read. Don't force any book. Make excursions to the library a learning time for you and the children.

In our family we recommend books to each other regularly and take opinions seriously. It's lonely not to have someone else share a

Each child has different interests; honor their choices.

book that has touched you in some way. Family closeness is not suddenly developed when children reach a certain age; it must begin from the first. A special joy comes when your small child says to you, "You'll love it," as he recommends Lois Lenski's *Little Train*.

One of my favorite memories involves just such a time of sharing a book. Traveling in Europe, we had purchased Elizabeth Goudge's *Little White Horse* for our twelve-year-old son to read. He enjoyed it so much he repeatedly said, "Mom, you've just got to read this book." One night I made the choice to spend the evening with him in our lodgings instead of attending an art lecture in Florence, Italy. I read *that* book. I was as delighted as he, and commented on incidents as I read. He was absorbed in his own book, but suddenly came over to my chair, gave me a tight hug, and said spontaneously, "I just had to tell you this minute that I love you!" I was taking time to enjoy his book. I treasure that evening. No art lecture could have done for us what sharing that book did, and later Father read it aloud to us again. (You'll be glad to know it is back in print now!)

When Roald Dahl's *Charlie and the Chocolate Factory* was first published, a teacher in our local school read it to her class. Children must have talked about it to their friends because seemingly half of the school came into the library to ask for the book. The librarian got the idea finally and ordered several copies. She said to me, "It isn't on *any* list, but I can't keep a copy on the shelves." Which all goes to show that children will like what they will, and I suspect that's how books get on lists. The success of the first Harry Potter book was a word-of-mouth publicity campaign by enthusiastic readers.

Every child in your family may not like every book in my book list. That would be expecting far too much. You may ask, "Why didn't she put this book on her list? We loved it." There wasn't room for them all. Keep it on your list and share the title with others. Expose your children to a variety of books, read some of the books aloud, but let the children ultimately decide what they enjoy.

Each child has different interests; honor their choices. Sometimes it is simply a matter of timing. Irene Hunt's *Up a Road Slowly* (1967 Newbery Medal) is a beautifully written story for a teenage girl who is by nature reflective and serious. It is a favorite book for many teenage girls, but saying, "This is good literature" will probably not make a carefree tomboy like it. Some good books that are just right for your child never make a list. *Charlotte's Web* did not win the top Newbery Medal, but millions of children think it is the best ever.

Wisdom demands that parents make some effort to understand both books and children.

Boys and girls go through a stage, usually around ten years of age, where they consume series books. In the past it was the Nancy Drew, Hardy Boys, or Sugar Creek Gang series; for others it was the Tarzan series. The Twin books by Lucy Fitch Perkins, the Mandie books by L. Leppard—the list could go on and on. Sometimes these are faddish, like the Goosebump books, which are pretty trivial. As of this writing *A Series of Unfortunate Events* by Lemony Snicket (a fictitious name?) have taken ten-year-olds by storm. In them the Baudelaire siblings find misfortune everywhere they turn. The stories are extremes in danger and outrage; seemingly the enemy is never defeated—all of which is both hilarious and fascinating. It is beyond truth and yet mysterious. Kids love them. (And they are quite clever!)

Few books in my book list are series books, but that is not because they are harmful. In general, they probably are not the best literature, but they meet a need and an interest in a child's life. Don't discourage the reading of series. Let a child read what he or she likes. At the right moment, be ready to recommend some others.

An Easy Way to Learn

Good literature teaches more than we know. Example always speaks louder than precept, and books can do more to inspire honor and tenacity of purpose than all the chiding and exhortations in the world.

The teaching is accumulative, too. One day our high schooler was discussing the whirlwind of destruction left behind by a couple of children visiting us. He said, "I got to thinking about how I would teach my children not to pull up wild flowers by the roots and destroy things, and then I wondered how I had learned myself. I decided I had learned from books to respect the world. In C. S. Lewis's books the animals and trees have personality; in pioneer stories Indians tried to walk through the forest without breaking a twig, and settlers respected the land; in Tolkien's books, the orcs are the bad guys who leave a path of careless destruction." He shrugged his shoulders as he concluded, "You put a whole childhood of reading together, and you don't have to take a conservation course."

From *The Book of Giant Stories* by David L. Harrison,
illustrated by Philippe Fix. Copyright © 1972 by Philippe Fix.
Used with permission of McGraw-Hill Book Company.

Chapter 4

Fantasy and Realism

Alice found herself falling mile after mile down the Rabbit's Hole until she thought she might be near the center of the earth. Presently she began to wonder if she would fall right through the earth.

"Well," thought Alice to herself, "after such a fall as this, I shall think nothing of tumbling down stairs."

Fantasy is like that. It makes "tumbling down stairs" relatively harmless. The very disparity between this magical world and ours somehow puts personal problems in perspective. I don't know quite how, but life seems more manageable and humankind more courageous after reading fantasy.

Well-written fantasy grabs the reader and gets him involved because it is, first of all, the simple pleasure of a good story. One meets characters of substance, like A. A. Milne's Winnie-the-Pooh with his honey and good humor, or the resourceful Mary Poppins, full of surprises, or the noble and courageous Frodo of The Lord of the Rings. The events of a fantasy are skillfully woven to create suspense and round the story off to a proper climax. Good fantasy meets the criteria of all good literature.

But there is more to good fantasy than that. It demands something extra of its readers; it asks them to pay attention. If one listens carefully, a second level of meaning often becomes obvious, and that, combined with the simple pleasure of a good story, makes the book

Good fantasy helps us see reality in unreality, credibility in incredibility.

worth reading over and over—worth reading at age ten and worth reading at fifty!

Reality in Unreality

Some people object and say that all those hidden meanings are lost on children. Lewis Mumford once said, "The words are for children, and the meanings are for men." That's not entirely true, but it is what makes fantasy attractive for all ages. Children suspect more is present than the actual story, and because there is little space between the real and the unreal world in a child's mind, they reach across with amazing ease and begin to ferret out the truth. They may read the story again years later and find that their experiences in life help them see more. Adults will read the same book and begin to better understand why they loved it as children. But at any age, a good fantasy provides an experience of quality and substance.

The most subtle and profound ideas are often found in books written for children. A kind of suspended reality exists in which what is true becomes more obvious. Good fantasy helps us see reality in unreality, credibility in incredibility. A child accepts and loves fantasy because of his own rich imagination and sense of wonder. For children, magical things are not nearly as complicated as they are for adults. They have room in their minds for all sorts of happenings. And those who write fantasy are not so much those who understand the heart of a child as those who have a child's heart themselves. Out of the depth of their personal experience they combine a child's heart with profound insights into life's meaning. Some fantasies laugh; some are full of nonsense; others are breathless with adventure and brave deeds. If you listen, you will hear more than the obvious story line.

For instance, back to the ridiculous events of *Alice in Wonderland*. The White Queen says, "The rule is, jam tomorrow, and jam yesterday—but never jam today."

"It must come sometimes to 'jam today,'" Alice objected.

"No, it can't," said the Queen. "It's jam every other day: today isn't any other day, you know."

"I don't understand you," said Alice. "It's dreadfully confusing."

But the reader is somehow amused, not confused. He appreciates the fantastic logic of the queen just as he understands Alice's matter-of-fact mind. Because life is sometimes like that. The language in the story is the language of nonsense, but at the same time there is an essence of truth contained in it. Perhaps that is why allusions to Alice are used again and again in literature and conversations. As the Red Queen said to Alice, "Even a joke should have some meaning."

Dragons and Unicorns

Not everyone takes to fantasies or fairy tales, although I believe most children do. These stories are certainly at their best when read aloud—especially fairy tales—because the lovely cadence of words and the economy of language make them a special experience. It is adults who worry over the make-believe, the magic, the strange creatures, the evil events, the wars, and sometimes the gore. Children have far less trouble. They readily know the difference between fantasy and reality. "No child confuses dragons or unicorns with cattle in a meadow," one writer said. It is the child who doesn't know about dragons and unicorns who is to be pitied!

I've never met a child (although there may be one) who has analyzed the emotional and physical impropriety of nursery rhymes like

> *There I met an old man*
> *Who would not say his prayers,*
> *I took him by the left leg*
> *And threw him down the stairs.*

That's simply a ludicrous scene and a good rhyme. Children don't squeeze life into boxes. They have room for a large variety of emotions and happenings and are quite aware of the possibilities in people. They know life is difficult; they are happy to believe it also turns out right in the end. I like *Beauty and the Beast* to this day because in that tale an act of love transforms what is ugly into something beautiful. I believe it still happens.

Bruno Bettelheim, a well-known child psychologist, contends that fairy tales provide children with an invaluable education in good and evil. He believes that all children have a rich supply of personal fantasies filled with fears and anxieties and that fairy tales reassure them and offer solutions. They learn how to deal constructively with their fears. Happy endings tell them that solutions and hope are real and model the kind of happy life children want to find. "Like all great art, fairy tales both delight and instruct; their special genius is that they do so in terms which speak directly to children."[1] Fairy tales, says Bettelheim, help children (and adults) answer such questions as: What

[1] Bruno Bettelheim, *The Uses of Encantment: The Meaning and Importance of Fairy Tales* (New York: Alfred A. Knopf, 1976), p. 53.

From *The Biggest Bear* by Lynd Ward. Copyright © 1952. Reproduced by permission of Houghton Mifflin Company.

is the world really like? How am I to live my life in it? How can I be myself?

While these metaphysical questions are handled in fairy tales and fantasies, they suggest rather than dictate answers. A good fantasy is not a thinly disguised moral message; it asks profound questions that develop out of the plot and the characters of the story. The word *fantasy* comes from the Greek and literally translated means "making visible." A proper story makes visible certain basic realities; it demonstrates options in handling life's situations.

For instance, sometimes we falter in the face of evil. We tell ourselves that we don't have all the information, and we excuse our personal indecision. Then we read a story and something inside us says yes, this is how we are to act. "How shall a man judge what to do in such times?" asks a character in The Lord of the Rings. "As he ever has judged," comes the reply. "Good and evil have not changed. It is man's part to discern them."

Our favorite fantasies are written by George MacDonald, C. S. Lewis, and J. R. R. Tolkien. (The British seem to have a corner on this market.) We have read C. S. Lewis's Narnia Chronicles (and his space trilogy) more often than any others. His vivid stories are filled with extraordinary events and familiar details. He expands our world with his view of loyalty, his differing concept of time, his logic, his view of truth, love, evil, and goodness—and the wonder of the imagination.

In a scene from *The Magician's Nephew* Lewis's characters explore dimensions of love and temptation and loyalty. Aslan, the golden-maned Lion (who is no ordinary lion), sends Digory and Polly, two children, to a faraway garden to get an apple to plant in the land of Narnia as a tree of protection. When they finally arrive at the place and Digory gets into the garden to pick the golden apple, he is confronted by a witch. She tells him that the apple gives youth and health to whoever eats it, and she encourages him to take one for himself and eat it. He is hungry, isn't he? Digory refuses, but he does remember his mother who is dying, and the witch urges him to take the apple to her. Aslan need never know. "Soon she will be quite well again. All will be well again. Your home will be happy again."

Digory gasps as if he has been hurt and puts his hand to his head, for he knows that the most terrible choice lies before him. The witch also suggests he leave Polly behind. At once all that the witch has been saying to him sounds false and hollow. He remembers the shining tears in Aslan's eyes and the promise he had made to Aslan. He returns to Narnia and walks straight up to Aslan, hands him the apple, and says, "I've brought you the apple you wanted, sir." "Well done," says Aslan in a voice that makes the earth shake.

Suddenly anything other than obedience and loyalty seems incredibly stupid. We have never read this story without feeling a profound longing to keep our promises and to do what is right—not because we have heard a sermon but because of the action and decisions of the characters in the story. I am convinced that fantasies quicken the ability to extract and apply principles in life as readers learn to make a transfer of ideas from allegory to reality. Good literature should always make life larger.

What Good Books Can Do

My friend Tracy Peterson, a teacher of English as a Second Language (ESL) for at-risk intermediate students, chose Katherine Paterson's fantasy *The King's Equal* for a class reading project. Published originally as a picture book, it is also published in novel form with short chapters and a splendid repetitive vocabulary. The plotline is simple: a dying king realizes that his arrogant son Raphael will soon inherit the throne, and in blessing him declares that Raphael will not receive the crown until he finds a wife who is his equal in beauty, wealth, and intelligence. Raphael's counselors, charged with finding this wife in one year, shake with fear because the prince has already declared himself superior to everyone in all three categories. How can they find someone he will accept as his equal?

In another part of the kingdom a childhood ago, a dying mother gave her daughter Rosamund her blessing that someday she would be a king's equal. Her circumstances make this highly unlikely, but when Raphael begins to destroy the kingdom with his greed, Rosamund, now a young woman, is sent by her father to the mountains to protect the family's goats, their last resource. There she befriends a wise wolf who shares her hut, and later gives her a golden circlet, telling her it is time to go to the city and present herself to the king as his equal. When they meet, Raphael knows he has found his heart's desire in Rosamund, but she quickly proves to be more than his equal! He must measure up and change his character to qualify to marry her. At Rosamund's urging, he goes to the mountain to be instructed by the same wolf. He changes into a humble, kind, caring man and returns one year later to claim Rosamund and marry her. (This is a bare-bones account of a wonderful tale!)

The classroom activities while reading this book varied from vocabulary and comprehension to journal entries and short essays. The students loved the story and saw things Tracy had not seen in it. Thirteen of the fourteen students were from animistic, non-western backgrounds, and were certain the wolf was Rosamund's mother. All of them wanted Tracy to ask Katherine Paterson to write more chapters for the story. One student with a gift for drawing said the story should have been a picture book. Imagine his delight when Tracy showed him the original publication as a picture book, complete with the lavish drawings of Vladimir Vagin.

But the most amazing response came from Teng, a student who had been on a downward course all year. He had changed from a sentimental boy to an angry gang member, fighting on the street and getting into trouble in school. Teng's journal responses were startling. He wrote about how disgusted he was with his life and behavior, and how he didn't know how to change. As the lowest reader in the class, he insisted that Tracy read to him so he wouldn't miss anything from the story.

Tracy tells Teng's story: "One day I called Teng out into the hall to talk privately with him. I asked him how he was going to deal with his dissatisfaction about his life. He said that he had made the (extremely dangerous) decision to leave the gang. I asked him why. He began telling me that some day he wanted to be equal to someone as lovely (inner beauty), wealthy (satisfied), and intelligent (wise) as Rosamund, and he would never qualify if he remained a gangster. We stood in the corridor crying with joy and fear while we considered Teng's situation. In a moment of utter eighth-grade stupidity, Teng had the gang's name tattooed on his upper right arm. It was huge, making him a target. We put together a plan to have the tattoo removed and, by the grace of God, Teng and I have been visiting a benevolent plastic surgeon monthly for the past year. I'm admittedly biased, but I think Teng could give the changed Raphael a run for his money."

Tracy continued, "I expect all my students to improve their reading and writing skills. I expect some of them to fall in love with great literature. But this was a dream come true—to fall in love with an ideal in a story and be changed."

Tracy noticed something else in the classroom: the vocabulary changed. Until this story, *cocky* was the most descriptive word students used. Now they began to use words from the story—*arrogant, vain,* or *greedy*. Rather than saying "the house of the king," they used *palace* and *castle* and talked about the *kingdom* or *domain*. Instead of *hard-working*, they could choose *industrious*. This new skill with words obviously helped their self-esteem.

Tracy's story from her classroom energized my already firm convictions. It beautifully illustrates the benefits that come from fine literature—words fitly spoken, characters memorable, a theme to challenge the heart—this is what we want for children!

And fantasy is not just for children. Some who have not grown old on the inside will always revel in it; others find their way into it as adults, maybe to escape a harsh world.

> *Words fitly spoken, characters memorable, a theme to challenge the heart—this is what we want for children!*

A Harsh Realism

After the upheaval in our society in the late 1960s, editors and writers became convinced that children needed "relevant books." Salesmen convinced bookstore buyers; librarians, eager to be contemporary, recommended them for reading. Someone once said that the worst features of an era are accented in the children's books of that period. Book by book our societal problems were dumped into children's books. What editors called "realism" is really adult betrayal, violence, sexual indiscretions, alcoholism, and the Big D's: death, divorce, disease, and drugs. Books with inconsequential plots and characters became thinly disguised "moralisms"—the kind of moralisms that come from a nonjudgmental culture urging readers to suspend judgment, to become understanding and noncondemning, and to realize their sexuality.

Paula Fox, a popular author of young adult novels, described what she felt authors were doing during this "realism" binge in an essay entitled "Bitter-Coated Sugar Pills":

> We offer sentimentalized information about copulation, tricked out with patronizing argot, as insulting to young readers as those "youth" movies ground out by aging filmmakers whose purpose, one knows, is not only high-minded but also passionately financial. At last we are letting the ignorant child in on the secret.
>
> Yet the real secret we keep to ourselves because we lack the courage and imagination to say it. It is the knowledge of what it is to be human, the knowledge that we are human from the first second we leap into the world and wail out our first breath. But that secret can only be revealed by the eternal mystery of the imagination, which works gaily with the most terrible truths.[2]

Some authors are still writing these kinds of books, but I believe the worst of this is over. Most young readers do not like these books. They call them "those gray books" and complain that, even if all this was true, it was too depressing to read about it. Richard Peck who wrote the heavy *Father Figure* story, full of dissonance and despair, has now written winners like *A Long Way from Chicago* and *A Year Down Yonder*, both delightful books. If you observe what books are winning the awards, you will see that editors are welcoming a new, more hopeful kind of book.

However, once a barrier is crossed, the gate is usually left open. Books for middle school readers today handle subjects once thought inappropriate. Profanity is less common than coarse language and demeaning four-letter words. The treatment of some subjects is explicit, vulgar, and inappropriate. It seems almost a plot to spoil childhood! A whole range of books have become "message books"— environmentalists and animal rights causes, and authors trying to make homosexuality an acceptable lifestyle. Editors are labeling some books for younger ages than the book warrants. Some books for "ten and up" should not be read until fifteen or older. Age-reading level on a book often becomes unreliable.

Defenders of these questionable books believe there is a need for candor because so many children feel isolated in their real-life sit-

[2]Paula Fox, "Bitter-Coated Sugar Pills," *Saturday Review*, 19 September 1970.

uations. Surely, they say, a young person reading stories about parents with excessive drinking problems would be comforted to know others share that problem. Safe and secure children from two-parent families in the suburbs need to know the problems of broken families in the inner city. For readers with no such experience, it gives understanding and compassion for others, they say.

On the surface that sounds convincing. Compassion and understanding are the by-products of good reading, and I'm heartily in favor of children having wider worlds than their own. Books give families a lot to talk about, giving us prime teaching opportunities. All good reading should accomplish this. But faddish books that exploit the permissiveness of our culture will not stand the test of time or of good literature.

A teacher friend reminded me that today's ten-year-olds are hardly innocent. Their parents take them to movies that handle subjects too adult for their years (where did the notion come from that adults are not adversely affected by what they see?); they watch almost anything they want on television at home. Young school children are now put through "lock-in drills" in their classrooms, a drill to teach them how to act if a shooting occurs in the school—a potential reality that causes everyone pain. That pushes children prematurely into a confusing world.

Knowing all this and more is true, I still maintain that reading should offer not just adventure, but the solace of hope and goodness, of another world where truth and right triumph. Good stories offer options to a child who may be caught in a destructive situation. That's why my teacher-friend Tracy's story enlivens my imagination.

Many authors and editors have turned the page on this negative kind of writing. Books like *Belle Prater's Boy* by Ruth White handle real families with real problems, but an underlying goodness and larger values support the story for middle school readers. *Out of the Dust* by Karen Hesse handles the poverty and hardship of the dustbowl years with grace and dignity, but still with more realism than most books did in the 1950s. The realism binge is leveling off in good ways.

Reading should offer the solace of hope and goodness, of another world where truth and right triumph.

An Emphasis on Significance

The question we need to ask of a story is this: does it illumine what is true in significant ways? Troubled and always in debt, Mr. Micawber in Dickens' *David Copperfield* is no paragon of virtue. Why are his

[3]Mary Hill Arbuthnot, *Children and Books* (Glenview, Ill.: Scott, Foresman and Co., 1964).

character and the details of his life so memorable? Can the reader understand or sympathize with the incredible complexities of Micawber's family life that result from his indiscretions? Characters like Mr. Micawber, Little Emily, and Uriah Heep are even somewhat shocking if you describe them out of context. Good literature does deal with reality, but not in the burdened way of recent years. Reality fairy tales are not morally superior to fantasy fairy tales.

A good book is not problem-centered; it is people-centered. It reveals how to be a human being and what the possibilities of life are; it offers hope.

Give me and my children a well-written story that—in the words of May Hill Arbuthnot in *Children and Books*—"reiterates the old verities that kindness and goodness will triumph over evil if they are backed by wisdom, wit and courage. These are basic truths we should like built into the depth of the child's consciousness."[3]

There is more—much more—than we have yet explored. Your children will want more than fantasy; give them fiction, nonfiction, historical fiction, and poetry. A good reading list like the bibliography at the back of this book will help you choose. Look for books like *The Door in the Wall; Bud, Not Buddy; Roll of Thunder, Hear My Cry; Ma Dear's Aprons; Blue Willow; The Hundred Dresses; The Rag Coat*—they are books that handle life and reality in the best possible way. Reality themes are not new in literature. Good literature has always dealt with truth, but not in a way that makes readers less. Good literature shows readers how to be more.

Chapter 5

Poetry

What is Poetry? Who knows?
Not the rose, but the scent of the rose;
Not the sky, but the light in the sky;
Not the fly, but the gleam of the fly;
Not the sea, but the sound of the sea;
Not myself, but what makes me
See, hear and feel something that prose
Cannot: and what it is, who knows!

ELEANOR FARJEON,
POEMS FOR CHILDREN

Poetry is a kind of verbal music. It is more than just doggerel that rhymes. It appeals more to feelings than to intellect. In poetry we get the shape and feel of words. Children may learn to appreciate poetry more than adults do because they are free to let it be what it is and not demand more of it.

Children first meet poetry in the repetitious rhythm of nursery rhymes. Most of them are nonsensical:

A pocketful of rye,
four-and-twenty blackbirds baked in a pie.

What a feathery idea!

Jack and Jill went up the hill
to fetch a pail of water.

Strange place to find a well!

But the sense really doesn't matter. In fact, I must confess that some poems which come most frequently to my mind are nonsensical ones from happy childhood memories. Their beat and verbal song seem to stick. That's why children often say when hearing nursery rhymes read, "Sing it again."

I have in my notebook an interesting quote (source unknown) that bears on the subject.

> Do you know what is wrong with people who never read nursery rhymes? I will tell you. When little boys and girls grow bigger and older, they should grow from the outside, leaving a little boy in the middle; even when they are quite grown up, the little child that once they were should be within them. But some unlucky people grow older from inside and so grow old through and through.

That has always seemed a dreadful fate to me.

The first poetry books (other than nursery rhymes) used at our house included A. A. Milne's *When We Were Very Young* and *Now We Are Six*. The poems vary from the nonsensical and eccentric to the warm and familiar. The contribution of Ernest Shepard's excellent illustrations add much to our enjoyment of these poems. Here are some excerpts:

They're changing the guard at Buckingham Palace—
Christopher Robin went down with Alice.
Alice is marrying one of the guard,
"A soldier's life is terrible hard,"
Says Alice.

or,

Ernest was an elephant, a great big fellow
Leonard was a lion with a six-foot tail,
George was a goat, and his beard was yellow,
And James was a very small snail.

From an appealing cadence such as this, what would you naturally name a stuffed lion or goat at your house?

Wouldn't you love to chant this one while taking a walk?

Whenever I walk in a London street,
I'm ever so careful to watch my feet,
And I keep in the squares
And the masses of bears
Who wait at the corners all ready to eat
The sillies who tread on the lines of the street,
Go back to their lairs
And I say to them, "Bears,
Just look how I'm walking in all of the squares!"

By all means give children generous doses of poets like A. A. Milne, Edward Lear, and Hilaire Belloc—just for fun.

Reading poetry is not the same as reading a story. Listening to poetry, a child becomes accustomed to words in an unfamiliar arrangement and to the cadence of the meter. Words "rise and fall and flow and pause and echo—like the singing of birds at daybreak or a little before the fall of night when daffodils take the winds of March with beauty," writes Walter de le Mare in *Tom Tiddler's Ground.*

There was an Old Man on
   whose nose
Most birds of the
   air could repose;
But they all flew away at the closing of day,
Which relieved that Old Man and his nose.

From *The Complete Nonsense Book* by Edward Lear.
Reprinted with permission of Dodd, Mead & Company.

Poetry is like music in that it has to have sound to be appreciated. Reading poetry aloud to a receptive child is one of the rewards of parenthood. The surprise and beauty of words may break on a child like the dawning of a fresh world, and he will be forever a lover of poetry.

Poems, like good seasonings, should be sprinkled lightly on the life of a child. One here, another delightful one there. Too much deadens the ability to hear and helps some children decide that poetry is wearisome. Boys and girls usually have a natural ear for poetry and a great capacity for enjoyment if the development of this kind of reading keeps pace with growth in other areas.

Lewis Gannett, who compiled *The Family Book of Verse*, writes, "When I was small, my father read poetry to the family at breakfast each morning, and on Sunday afternoons he read longer poetry to those who came to listen. I seem to recall sometimes resenting the morning delay before eating . . . yet, rereading old poems . . . again and again I seem to be hearing—and appreciating—echoes of my father's voice. I observe that my daughter reads every night—sometimes poetry—to her six daughters and they obviously enjoy it. It would be a proud boast if this book should help encourage the old custom of reading poetry aloud at home."

I include Gannett's comments for obvious reasons. Your children may not coax you to read a poem. Sometimes when you are bent upon sharing one, they may give you a look of patient endurance. But valuable experiences are not always appreciated at the time; later they yield their rewards. We do many things for our families because we decide they are *right* to do. The spirit, the attitude, the sense of adventure with which they are done makes all the difference! And I have often seen in our house a warm look of love that says secretly, "This is my dad!" when my husband reads a poem, introducing it with, "My dad used to read this to us."

Of course, you'll want to read some from Robert Louis Stevenson's *A Child's Garden of Verses* for warmth of childhood pleasures.

> *A birdie with a yellow bill*
> *Hopped upon the window sill.*
> *Cocked his shining eye and said,*
> *"Ain't you 'shamed, you sleepy-head?"*

My own father used to awaken me with those words.
Or do you remember:

I saw you toss the kites on high
And blow the birds about the sky;
And all around I heard you pass
Like ladies' skirts across the grass—
O wind, a-blowing all day long,
O wind, that sings so loud a song!

Eleanor Farjeon's poetry for children has a wit and melody all its own. Sounds and senses are accentuated in the poetry of Carl Sandburg and Robert Frost. Here is Frost's "The Pasture":

I'm going out to clean the pasture spring;
I'll only stop to rake the leaves away
(And wait to watch the water clear, I may):
I sha'n't be gone long—You come too.
I'm going out to fetch the little calf
That's standing by the mother. It's so young,
It totters when she licks it with her tongue.
I sha'n't be gone long—You come too.

Feel Carl Sandburg's "Fog":

The fog comes
on little cat feet.
It sits looking
over harbor and city
on silent haunches
and then moves on.

Sara Teasdale and Christina Rossetti often wrote about nature. Older children feel in their hearts what Sara Teasdale shared in this excerpt from "Barter":

Life has loveliness to sell—
All beautiful and splendid things,
Blue waves whitened on a cliff,
Soaring fire that sways and sings,
And children's faces looking up
Holding wonder like a cup.

Each poet brings his or her own style and emotional wealth to the poem. Anthologies give us the best opportunity to sample many flavors of poetry. Several of these are listed in the bibliography.

When you are first introducing poetry to a child, you will use happy verse—nonsensical, exaggerated, cozy—whatever you choose. As children grow older, don't shy away from poetry which you may think is too deep or too sad for them. Trust children to understand more than they can express. They may or may not say to you, "That poem understands me," but that may be what they feel inside. Many children are inspired to write their own poems from experiences like these.

Listen to the mood of Edna St. Vincent Millay's "God's World":

O world, I cannot hold thee close enough!
Thy winds, thy wide gray skies!
Thy mists that roll and rise!
Thy woods, this autumn day, that ache and sag
And all but cry with color!

Or Emily Dickinson's "Have You Got a Brook?"

Have you got a brook in your little heart,
Where bashful flowers blow,
And blushing birds go down to drink
And shadows tremble so?
And nobody knows, so still it flows,
That any brook is there;
And yet your little draught of life
Is daily drunken there.

By all means, share old favorites like Longfellow's "Paul Revere's Ride":

Listen, my children, and you shall hear
Of the midnight ride of Paul Revere,
On the eighteenth of April, in Seventy-five;
Hardly a man is now alive
Who remembers that famous day and year.

Or the romance of Alfred Noyes' "The Highwayman":

The wind was a torrent of darkness among the gusty trees,
The moon was a ghostly galleon tossed upon cloudy seas,
The road was a ribbon of moonlight over the purple moor,
And the highwayman came riding—
Riding—riding—
The highwayman came riding, up to the old inn door.

Samuel Taylor Coleridge's "The Rime of the Ancient Mariner" will stir the heart of children entering their teens. I remember feeling very thirsty when hearing this haunting tale.

> *Water, water everywhere,*
> *And all the boards did shrink;*
> *Water, water everywhere,*
> *Nor any drop to drink.*

Samuel Butler once remarked that this poem would not have taken off so well if it had been called "The Old Sailor," a thought that makes me smile. Butler may well be right about the romance of its title, but Coleridge has other stirring poems with less romantic titles. Read his "Christabel" and "Kubla Khan," so rich in imagination.

The list extends endlessly for these golden oldies, for there are so many to be met and enjoyed—William Blake, e. e. cummings, John Donne, Kipling, and others. Do you remember hearing "Sea-Fever"?

> *I must go down to the seas again, to the lonely sea and the sky,*
> *And all I ask is a tall ship and a star to steer her by.*

This song of the sea was written by John Masefield, who also penned a magnificent Christian poem, "The Everlasting Mercy," one you will want to share with your older children.

One can hardly forget Francis Thompson's "The Hound of Heaven," portraying so vividly man's flight from God:

> *I fled Him, down the nights and down the days;*
> *I fled Him, down the arches of the years.*

It's a great spiritual experience to share with your children. But long before they are old enough to understand the fascinating account of "The Hound of Heaven," they ought to meet Francis Thompson in "Ex Ore Infantium," one of my favorites:

> *Little Jesus, wast Thou shy*
> *Once, and just so small as I?*
> *And what did it feel like to be*
> *Out of heaven, and just like me?*

Ernest Thayer's "Casey at the Bat" or Robert Service's "The Cremation of Sam McGee" have none of the mystical imagery of other verse but will capture the imagination of some. Explore, take time out to browse through good anthologies for children, and find some new poems to enjoy yourself.

The Psalms are rich in poetic melody, like this first verse from Psalm 91.

He who dwells in the shelter of the Most High,
Will rest in the shadow of the Almighty,
I will say of the Lord, "He is my refuge and my fortress;
My God, in whom I trust."

After you've read about the Red Sea incident, enjoy that wonderful song of Moses in Exodus 15:

I will sing to the Lord,
for he is highly exalted.
The horse and his rider
he has hurled into the sea.

When reading of David's sin with Bathsheba, include Psalm 51:

Have mercy on me, O God,
According to your unfailing love;
According to your great compassion
blot out my transgressions.

Picture old Moses, the man of God, leading the children of Israel, and saying to the Lord in Psalm 90,

Lord, you have been our dwelling place throughout
*   all generations.*
Before the mountains were born or you brought forth
*   the earth and the world,*
From everlasting to everlasting you are God.

Jeremiah captures humankind's perpetual wandering in his second chapter:

For my people have committed two sins;
they have forsaken me,
the spring of living water,
and have dug their own cisterns,
broken cisterns,
that cannot hold water.

You will notice I have stuck closely to old favorites in this chapter on poetry, but that is not without purpose. They are favorites because people have loved them, and this is a good place to begin.

Their lines sing, and their content is not obscure. As you move on into the world of poetry, you will find unfamiliar meter and blank verse, an irregular kind of prose called poetry. Don't be afraid to try it; it may fit your mood very well.

If you share poetry with your children, someday you will know the delight of your children sharing favorites with you. I picked up our ninth grader one afternoon after school to take him to the barbershop for a haircut. As he got out of the car, he reached into the back pocket of his jeans and drew out a sheet of notebook paper, folded many times, saying, "We studied this in school today, and I thought you'd like it." While he was getting his haircut, I sat in the car and read what he had bothered to copy for my enjoyment, a poem by James Russell Lowell:

> *They are the slaves who fear to speak*
> *For the fallen and the weak;*
> *They are the slaves who will not choose*
> *Hatred, scoffing and abuse,*
> *Rather than in silence shrink*
> *From the truth they needs must think;*
> *They are the slaves who dare not be*
> *In the right with two or three.*

Sharing makes for lovely companionship.

From *Sam, Bangs, and Moonshine*, written and illustrated
by Evaline Ness. Copyright © 1966 by Evaline Ness. Reproduced
by permission of Holt, Rinehart and Winston, Publishers.

Chapter 6

The Pleasure of
a Shared Adventure

If families don't read books together, how do they know each other's friends?"

That's exactly how we feel about it.

Reading aloud as a family has bound us together, as sharing an adventure always does. We know the same people. We have gone through emotional crises together as we felt anger, sadness, fear, gladness, and tenderness in the world of the book we were reading. Something happens to us that is better experienced than described—a kind of enlarging of heart—when we encounter passages full of grand language and noble thoughts.

Much of our secret family idioms come from the books we have read together. I say "secret" because a specialness surrounds it. You need to have shared the book to know what the phrase means, and when we use it, it's communication of the heart.

Sometimes it is silly doggerel like Horton's declaration of faithfulness in Dr. Seuss's *Horton Hatches an Egg*:

I meant what I said
And I said what I meant,
An elephant is faithful
One hundred percent.

Other times we speak of *Narnian air, the Ents, Barkis is willin', a useful pot for putting things in,* and hundreds of like phrases. When we went to visit a favorite spot and saw that much of what we remembered as beautiful had changed, our son said, "The orcs have been here," and we didn't need to say more.

We don't read a book to get a family vocabulary, you understand. It is just a cozy by-product worth mentioning only because of the intimacy of experience it expresses. That's the important part.

Using Books to Communicate

Not infrequently parents complain of an inability to communicate with their children. "I cannot understand how he thinks!" I want to ask if they ever *really* thought together about ideas. Parents may treat children as *children* most of their lives—giving them "milk," working hard to provide opportunities for them—and then suddenly the children are on the verge of adulthood and their parents have never become acquainted with them as *people.* It *is* frightening to suddenly find people living in your household whom you don't know!

You can't one day decide to know your children and have it magically happen. You begin from the beginning by sharing "the honey" of life, as well as providing "the milk." Knowing someone means sharing ideas, growing together. It means not being embarrassed about feelings or being yourself. As a small boy, our son frequently commented, "I like him. He treats me like I'm a people." It became a family saying; being treated like "a people" means being taken seriously and being liked for who you really are. Interpersonal relationships within a family develop on this level.

At the age of seventy, Laurence Housman writes about the contribution reading made in his family in *The Unexpected Years:*

> These family readings formed so satisfying a bond between older and younger that I can hardly think of family life without it; and I marvel when I hear of families in whose upbringing it has had no place.

In this day of committees and television, we don't marvel as Mr. Housman does, but we do recommend family reading with great enthusiasm, for we have seen what it has done for our family and the immense pleasure and richness it has brought. Finishing the last book of Tolkien's trilogy was some of the most exciting reading we've ever done. A trip by car across the state became especially delicious because we were able to get extra chapters read as we drove along together. We share Mr. Housman's sentiments.

Reading Good Stories Aloud

Family reading aloud demands good literature. Only the best can stand the test of having the words hit the airwaves and fall into the minds of such a variety of ages. You won't find busy parents (especially fathers) reading insipid, sentimental stories aloud for very long—and the best family reading includes a father's voice. That's a fact, however, not an excuse. My husband's work demanded that he travel, sometimes as much as fifty percent of the time. We kept a special book we only read when he was home, and another that we read when he was gone. But we always felt compelled to give him great, long summaries of what we were reading so he wouldn't feel left out!

At the outset, with child number one, begin with the simple but good stories that were favorites in your own childhood or that you've recently discovered. While the plot may not hold you as adults, something about it seems to come alive with freshness and gives what someone described as "a springtime urge to make them more beguiling than they ever sounded before."

Soon stories move into quite another class because children can understand far more than is sometimes guessed. When child number two comes along and is big enough to join the reading circle, if the favorites have been special literature they bear repeating, and no one minds. Each child deserves some catching up along the way, but do keep moving on up.

If you have children ages five to twelve, read aloud together with the two older children in mind. The youngest, even if she doesn't always understand, feels the comfortable security of the parent's voice and of being included in the "inner circle." Sometimes she falls asleep in her father's arms, but she would rather be there with the family than in bed alone. Not infrequently the older children take special pleasure in rereading past favorites with the younger ones, a good kind of sharing.

"A book read aloud is a book better remembered, especially if the reading took place in childhood," writes William Henry Chamberlain in *Saturday Review.* "One of the first books my father read to me was that old, romantic war horse, *Ivanhoe,* by Sir Walter Scott. It has been decades since I last picked it up; but my memory, even for quite trivial incidents, is still quite keen. I can almost reconstruct from memory the language of the scene where a haughty Norman baron exclaims derogatorily, 'Your Highness may call me a Saxon!' to receive a prompt rebuff from stout old Cedric, the father of Ivanhoe, 'Who calls thee a Saxon will do thee an honor as great as it is undeserved.'"

Reading aloud doesn't allow anyone to set a speed record, but this is one of its advantages. How nice to amble together through the descriptive paragraphs, which might otherwise be raced past, and take a leisurely look around. Everyone sees and feels more this way.

Characters seem more real when a story is read with some gift of expression. Maybe it is because a whole family is identifying with the characters and this strengthens the bonds one feels. Beautiful writing can almost break your hearts as you see how words are meant to be used. More adult children begin to interject, "That is magnificent!" or "What terrific insight!" And sometimes the reader gets such a large lump in his throat over the beauty or pathos of a situation that we all pause to swallow back our agony before going on. Who can read of Sidney Carton's vision of the future before he goes off to the guillotine in *A Tale of Two Cities* without a tear? Or of Billy's relationship with his dog in Wilson Rawls' *Where the Red Fern Grows* without emotion? Or the crisis in Daniel's life in Elizabeth George Speare's *The Bronze Bow* without having to swallow down the lump in your throat?

Great Read-Aloud Books

I've already mentioned some of our favorite read-aloud books, but don't let these suggestions keep you from discovering others. We've read *Winnie-the-Pooh* more times than anyone would believe. Pooh books have a kind of wisdom and humor that gets better with the years. All of his friends are like people we know. As Poohphiles, we play Pooh Sticks on the bridge, we've gone on many an "expotition" to the North Pole, and we have wished to unbounce many a Tigger. It's cheating older children to list A. A. Milne's classic under a five-to-nine age bracket. You have to be older to get the humor. Pooh is a collegiate favorite!

Topping our best-reading list are the seven children's books by C. S. Lewis—the Narnia books, we call them. These seven gems have delighted us numerous times, each fresh reading providing new insights. What makes them so special? Excellent weaving of plot and characters into a most exciting, imaginative series of adventures, with the masterful skill of C. S. Lewis's style. But even more than this: the quality of the theme behind the stories!

The Narnia books are rich in allegory, but apart from the allegory, the books stand as superbly written adventure stories, and schoolteachers have held their classes spellbound with them without ever alluding to the allegory. Yet it is the allegory that has added the plus of pleasure for our family.

Let your children find the allegory; don't scoop the story for them.

When Aslan, the golden-maned lion is captured by the witch, shorn of his majestic mane, tormented, and finally killed, let your children ache with the sadness of the four children in the story. When Aslan comes bounding over the hill the next morning, they will know the same joy as the children in the story. What a wonderful moment!

Each time we finished one book we were sure the next in the series couldn't be as good. When we read *The Last Battle*, we felt we had been introduced to the most creative thinking about heaven we had ever done. Imagine running with a unicorn and never getting tired, or even running up a waterfall! If this sounds insane to you, then you'll have to read the book, and I hope you do.

The Wind in the Willows by Kenneth Grahame has been loved by children and adults for nearly a hundred years. Sometime around your child's tenth birthday, you ought to read it aloud together. Read it again for twelve-year-olds or

Illustration by Ernest H. Shepard (copyright © 1933 Charles Scribner's Sons, renewal copyright © 1961 Ernest H. Shepard) reproduced with the permission of Charles Scribner's Sons from *The Wind in the Willows*, page 92, by Kenneth Grahame.

sixteen-year-olds. The book gets better as one gets older. Last summer a friend and her college-graduate daughter sat by the river in

England and read the book aloud again. The fellowship of Rat, who likes to mess around in boats, Mole with his wisdom, and the erratic Mr. Toad is too good to miss. Here again is an enduring quality of writing, rich in feeling and the author's commitment to the world he creates. When Ernest Shepard illustrated the story, he visited Kenneth Grahame in England, walking along the riverbank to make sketches of the setting for the story. "I love these little people," said Grahame. "Be kind to them. Make them real." And they do become real as you meet them in the story, and their sayings will surely become part of your family idioms. Who can forget the Christmas scene at Mole End, with the little mice, red mufflers wrapped around their throats, standing in a semicircle outside, singing,

> *Villagers all, this frosty tide*
> *Let your doors swing open wide.*

If you are looking for children's books that have strong moral and Christian emphasis, the books of Patricia St. John are wonderful finds. Her *Treasures of the Snow* and *Star of Light* are two of my favorites.

George MacDonald profoundly influenced C. S. Lewis, and he will profoundly influence your family as well. *The Princess and the Goblin, The Princess and Curdie*, and *At the Back of the North Wind* all have a supernatural touch. In *The Light Princess* we meet a girl who cannot participate in real life because she has no gravity. She is rescued when someone loves her enough to die for her. Adults enjoy George MacDonald's books as much as children because they see more in the story. Rich in wisdom, they are books your family will want to investigate.

I like reading aloud books from the classic book list because their excellent use of language is showcased. Some of the sentences and descriptions are so well constructed that you can afford to stop and marvel a bit over the beauty. The descriptions and character details may sometimes discourage children to read them individually, but together with a good reader such a book can soar. And there is so much to talk about.

When our son was twelve we began reading *David Copperfield, Oliver Twist*, and eventually *A Tale of Two Cities* aloud as a family. Charles Dickens' characters are magnificent; we *know* Wilkins Micawber, Lil' Emily, Peggotty, Uriah Heep, Oliver, and all the others. We didn't discuss these books as classics; we simply read them and enjoyed them.

At one point we read the unabridged edition of *Robinson Crusoe* together. My husband's freshman poetry teacher sent it to our son

Mark as a gift, but it became a gift for my husband and me as well, because we had never read this as Defoe wrote it. We were surprised that a condensation had cheated us out of so much—even the seemingly dreary passages which describe the hopelessness of Crusoe's future on the island. Then one day Crusoe discovered a Bible in the bottom of an old trunk, and we saw the man we had known only as a shipwrecked victim become a different man. No child listening to this story could miss the convincing difference Crusoe's conversion made in his view of the island and life.

But do be wise in your choice of books. Don't force your children to appreciate any of these books. There are too many other good books to choose from which may meet their needs and yours more fully. Reading should be fun.

Reading J. R. R. Tolkien's *The Hobbit* and The Lord of the Rings series has been an experience, and we have read it many times. Here is a masterful spinner of tales! We are awed by the power of language, the depth of characterization, the force of adventure. The test of good writing is the quality of the experience we receive in reading it. This is great writing! By all means, read Tolkien. (Look in the library for Books-on-Tape, Rob Inglis reading the Tolkien trilogy aloud. It's the best!)

We finished the last book of the Tolkien trilogy, *The Return of the King*, on a wilderness canoe trip in the Canadian bush. One morning when the wind was cold and strong, we huddled together in the largest tent to read. We were at such an exciting point in the book that it was easy to go on for several chapters. The tale was reaching its climax, the reader was having difficulty with the lump in his throat, and all of us had wet eyes over the sheer beauty of the scene of triumph after the destruction of the evil ring. If you have read the book, can you still feel with us the fulfillment of victory, of utter joy as the King comes into his own rightful place and all his warriors are honored?

> And all the host laughed and wept, and in the midst of their merriment and tears the clear voice of the minstrel rose like silver and gold, and all men were hushed. And he sang to them, now in the Elven-tongue, now in the speech of the West, until their hearts, wounded with sweet words, overflowed, and their joy was like swords, and they passed in thought out to regions where pain and delight flow together and tears are the very wine of blessedness.[1]

Later, when we said good-night and prayed together by a moonlit shore, a seventeen-year-old thanked God not just for "beautiful things we can see, but for beautiful words which remind us of realities we cannot see."

The test of good writing is the quality of the experience we receive in reading it.

[1] J. R. R. Tolkien, *The Return of the King* (New York: Balantine, 1976), p. 286.

> *Good books provide support for the kind of character we hope to see developed in our children.*

Good Books Are Good Teachers

I have mentioned two of the by-products of reading aloud: family closeness because of a shared experience and the bond of appreciation of good writing. The third factor has been alluded to: the opportunity of teaching what is true and good.

Cruelty, evil, and greed come into clear focus against kindness, truth, and honor in a well-written story. I say *well-written* because nothing offends a child more than having to be told when something is mean and base or noble and good. This painful spelling out of what one is supposed to learn from a story evidences the author's inability to create valid characters in a real-life plot. And it insults children.

The best teaching we have done in our family has been through reading the Bible and good books aloud together. It is really not such a profound concept. How would you best be enlightened to some truth? Is it by being told that it was wrong to be nasty and thoughtless to others, or to meet and come to love some character in a story and then feel her hurts when someone is unkind and says cruel things?

We sometimes talk about the characters we meet in our stories and about the motivation behind their deeds. We discuss worthy ideas and try to hang important concepts onto a larger framework of truth. Good books fulfill our human need for adventure and wider experience, but they also provide support for the kind of character we hope to see developed in our children.

Reading *The Adventures of Robin Hood*, we discussed some pretty important issues when a tearful child asked, "Did Robin Hood go to heaven? He was such a good man." We didn't completely solve our mutual sorrow over Robin's death in the story, but some weightier matters were touched upon.

But deeper than this have been those elements of great strength of character and largeness of heart that I spoke of earlier. These are intangible things. One cannot drive a point home and say, "There he has learned that lesson." But by continual exposure to a variety of people and experiences, the real values of life are taught most profoundly. What we are doing is helping our children collect "bits of perfection" of ideas and values on which to build their lives.

Again, I recall a quote of Paul Hazard: "I like books that set in action truths worthy of lasting forever, and of inspiring one's whole inner life."

What a pleasure to share that kind of a book with a child!

Chapter 7

Honey from the Rock

My grandfather was a Dutch immigrant with ten children. He and Grandmother took seriously the instructions God gave Moses for the children of Israel in Deuteronomy 6:6–7, believing this to be a parent's responsibility:

> These commandments that I give you today are to be upon your hearts. Impress them on your children. Talk about them when you sit at home and when you walk along the road, when you lie down and when you get up.

As the family gathered around the table for meals, one of my grandparents read from the Bible. It was a kind of spiritual dessert. They had enjoyed physical food from the hand of God; now they would enjoy spiritual food.

My father was one of these children. Later, when his four offspring sat around his table, he initiated the same practice. (As far as I know, his brothers and sisters have done similarly in their homes.) We never discussed whether or not we wanted to do this; it was just always done and never, to my knowledge, questioned. Reading material was chosen according to our ages. Often at the evening meal we read from a Bible storybook, but at least once a day we read short selections from the Bible. For some reason we read Proverbs more than any other single book; my parents must have believed that book contained an extraordinary amount of wisdom for everyday living.

To the children in our family this was a logical thing for a family to do. No one left the table, unless for special reasons, until we read the Scriptures together. This was no legalistic ritual; it was family habit. Thinking back, I remember numerous instances when our friends called for us and we asked them to wait until we had finished dinner. Dessert may have been served, but none of us considered the meal finished until we had read together.

As I recounted this to a group of young couples recently, one father asked me, "Didn't you all grow up resenting your father and Christianity?" I felt an aching kind of amusement at his question.

It was quite the other way around! In all honesty, I could say that our parents and memories of family life are extra dear because of this. Four new families have come out of our parental home, involving fourteen more children. Each family follows the pattern we learned at home. Our expectations are that each of these fourteen will pursue a similar practice in their homes in years to come.

I smile when I visit my brothers' homes and hear them stop in the middle of the reading to ask a child they suspect is not listening, "David, what was the last word?" That's what my father used to do. It will be fun to see if the grandsons use the same device on their children.

Why is it that family Bible reading is such a rare thing in today's homes, especially when the Bible is the most alive, pertinent book in the world? Why did that young father expect that disciplined Scripture reading would produce resentment? Let me suggest several reasons.

No Phony Performances

Too many people have a phony image of what this involves. Their minds conjure up pictures of a "family altar" with a large open Bible on the table against a background of flowers or a picture of Jesus. Around this scene, the family is piously kneeling for a minor church service each night. The people seem unreal, the language is that of Zion, and the experience looks as painful as possible.

But that image is a pretty shabby excuse for not making the Bible a central book in our homes. We can shout against the abuses of false piety, but that is hardly a creative exercise and a pretty shabby excuse for not doing something more genuine. We need less reaction, fewer excuses, and some positive action if our families are going to stand the test of an increasingly secular world.

Second, parents may not be really convinced of the importance of biblical instruction. We generally do arrange for what we believe is important. Life is never so busy that we don't manage to see that our family has nourishing food, adequate clothing, and proper sleep—and all the busy extras of life, even Sunday school.

But parents who never read the Bible outside of an organized meeting of the church are not likely to sense the urgency of instructing children in the most important truth in the world. If we really believe that God speaks through this book, how can we possibly handle it so carelessly and leave the responsibility for its content to someone else?

What is probably lacking the most is the discipline that makes family life work. Parents need to live their lives with conviction, not hesitation. If you must make a fresh decision each day *whether* you will read the Scriptures and *when* you will read them, the Bible will probably not be read very often. Increasingly, the family life of believers has little to distinguish it from secular family life.

Eating together and giving thanks for daily mercies should be a basic feature of

The goat who wanted to become a lion.

From *Jungle Doctor's Monkey Tales* by Paul White, illustrated by Graham Wade. Copyright © 1957, The Paternoster Press: used by permission.

our home life. In a discussion-growth group someone asked, "What was your favorite room in your family home?" I said without hesitation, "The breakfast room." That is where we ate our meals together as a family. We talked about the day, about our burning ideas, and shared our new jokes. Often one of our parents had to keep order by giving permission to speak because we all wanted to talk at once. No one left the table as soon as he had finished his food. Of course, I've already said that we read briefly at the close of the meal, but leaving

Parents must decide what quality of family life they will have and then use the necessary discipline to accomplish this.

would also mean that I didn't care what my brother was planning to do or what happened in my sister's day, an unthinkable lack of courtesy. Naturally we were nasty to each other or restless on occasions, but this didn't change our overall family pattern.

Eating Together as a Family

I sense there is something sacred about eating together as a family. Sharing a meal with others is part of the hospitality and belonging to each other that we read about in the Bible. Where do our children learn what it means "to practice hospitality" if it isn't around our own table, in our own home, with our own family? We give thanks together, we eat together, we talk together. It seems natural that we should read the Bible together. You may decide another time works better for you than mealtime; I only recommend this because I have seen it stand the test of three generations. It is a workable plan.

Breakfast-time best suits our family for Bible reading. (We usually are reading another book after dinner.) When I dropped in at my sister's home just as they were finishing dinner, I was in time to join them for their Bible reading—five sons around the table. The evening meal works best for them.

Interestingly, we often reproduce in our homes the pattern we knew as children. Even those who complain bitterly about the deficiencies of their childhood family life often reproduce a pattern not noticeably different from the one against which they chafed. Others swing a full 180 degrees away from the past. Whether this is wisdom or rebellion depends on the quality of the motivation and the goals that are set.

Parents *must* decide what quality of family life they will have and then use the necessary discipline to accomplish this. Otherwise life will push the family in diverse directions, and they will be victims rather than disciples.

Ask a child if he wants to read the Bible after breakfast, and he may say *no*. Build it into the routine as naturally as drinking orange juice, and he will get proper nourishment. One of my favorite cartoons shows a child in a progressive school commenting to his teacher, "You mean *I* have to decide what I want to do?" When you are small and don't know what is valuable, that is an agonizing responsibility to place on a child.

Overcoming Obstacles

I have mentioned hindrances to family instruction at length because obstacles need to be faced honestly. It isn't enough to say, "Teach your children what the Bible says," thus adding to the burden of guilt parents already feel. Parents may not know how to begin. Isolating the problem is part of the solution.

Some time ago I listened to a panel of concerned parents discuss challenges to family life today. Several on the panel mentioned their appreciation of the biblical background given them by their parents. Yet not one of the families was successfully having any kind of regular biblical instruction in their own homes. Their reasons will sound familiar.

> *They wiggle and squirm so much that we wonder what they get out of it anyway.*
> *We are just never all together when there is enough time.*
> *We have decided to wait until the children are older and want to participate more willingly.*
> *We try to do something special every now and then.*

I listened and thought of my grandparents. With ten children I'm sure it wasn't always convenient to read the Bible, and there was plenty of wiggling. Grandfather probably didn't stop to psychoanalyze; he just did what he felt needed doing. I felt a rush of gratitude for such a consistent heritage. Because Grandfather was faithful, my father was faithful, and we grew up in a home where we knew the importance and authority of the Bible. We not only have a heritage; we are giving our children one. We decide what kind it will be.

But what if the father doesn't take any leadership to help make this happen? What if he is away from home much of the time? What if the mother works late? What if soccer practice interferes? Many families flounder because of societal patterns. Don't cancel something as important as Bible reading while waiting for more ideal circumstances. A child's life is too brief! Not to carry on with something as vital to life as this is tantamount to saying, "We won't eat any meals because Dad isn't with us."

I must confess to a personal reaction against the words *family devotions* or *family altar*. Maybe it is because these terms have a sentimental, somewhat unreal flavor. The realities of our faith do not require an "altar." "Devotion" is not turned on during a family reading time if we don't have it as a reality all day long. I want to build more content into this family time than these words allow me personally. But what we call it isn't as important as that we do it! So we simply refer to it as Bible reading.

But enough discussion about hang-ups which hinder us. Let's go on to a clear idea of our goal in Bible reading. Why is it so important? What are some meaningful ways to accomplish it?

The Goal

The goal of family Bible reading is to teach children to think biblically.

That's a large goal: *to think biblically*. It means a good bit more than quoting certain Scripture verses or participating in quizzes. It involves squaring up our thinking with what the Bible says about God, about man, about sin, about redemption, about human need, and about righteousness. Thinking biblically insists on an understanding of the vast sweep of what Scripture reveals to us. It is the gauge against which we measure our ideas and our lives.

How has God worked in human history? What is his goal? What is his essential nature, his character? What is the nature of human beings? What are their basic needs? How does the death of Jesus Christ fit into the picture? How do we know what is true? These are only some of the questions we answer in learning to think biblically.

The ability to quote salvation or assurance verses is inadequate unless the verses fit into a larger concept of the character of God and an understanding of his righteousness. Knowing favorite biblical heroes and specific stories becomes most meaningful when fit into a larger view of what their lives demonstrate about people or about God's character.

Parents, not uncommonly, invest time with small children, reading them favorite Bible stories and speaking of salvation. The failure comes in teaching children through their teens how this information fits together to form a true basis for life. Our goal is a valid world/life view. This cannot be scolded into a person; we can only expose young minds to great truth and discuss it with them. Whether a child adopts a Christian world/life view is not our responsibility. Our job is to expose the child to what we believe is true. (See *Honey for a Teen's Heart* for a larger treatment of reading the Bible with teens.)

Our need for a word from God is never finished. He speaks to our situation, ministers to our problem areas. We receive fresh insights, daily reminders, and new promises because the Bible is indeed profitable "for teaching, rebuking, correcting and training in righteousness" (2 Timothy 3:16).

    We demonstrate our confidence in the authority of the Bible as the Word of God by the way we use it in our homes and by our personal obedience to it. No amount of emotional, cozy feeling will stand the rigorous test of exposure to secular culture. Our faith has intellectual content; we must know what we believe. Emotional warmth flows out of the application and obedience of these great truths.

Our faith has intellectual content; we must know what we believe.

Attaining the Goal

Begin early to teach your children about God and his Son by reading together from Bible storybooks that fit your child's age. Stories that relate biblical teaching to real life give opportunity for in-depth discovery as children grow. Often questions at the end of the story give children the fun of remembering and taking turns. Never before have publishers offered such creative full-color books, good writing, and excellent graphics. You'll find yourself learning afresh as you teach your children.

    I'd like to share the idea that has worked best toward attaining the goal in our family life. We have given this simple method years of trial and are pleased with its effectiveness in making the Bible meaningful.

    We began with four-year-old Mark to read aloud from the Gospel of Mark. We chose this Gospel because of its short narrative passages and incidentally because it was called *Mark*. Father had a plan: Everyone at the table (and this included our numerous guests) had to ask a question and answer one.

    We made a game out of it: sometimes the question was directed to the person on our left, other times to the person on our right. We'd have to listen carefully, because sometimes the question we had thought to ask was usurped by someone whose turn came first, and we would have to think of another.

    At first our questions were simple. *Where did Jesus go? What did Jesus do? Who went with Jesus?* Children pick up the idea rapidly.

    Then we began to interject another kind of question. *Why did Jesus say that? What does he mean?*

    And then, *What can we learn from Jesus about the way we ought to act?*

*No need to attempt
to protect truth,
to explain away
seeming
inconsistencies
either.*

In these questions are the three elements which open up any text: FACT—what does it say? INTERPRETATION—what does it mean? APPLICATION—what does it mean to me?

Children's questions invariably center on facts, but before long you will find them asking deeply penetrating ones. *If Jesus could raise Lazarus from the dead, why did he let his dear friend John the Baptist stay dead? Why did the Jews say Jesus had an evil spirit?* Increasingly we delved into the meat of what the text was saying.

Mark was delighted when his father introduced a two-part question, and thereupon set out to explore the possibility of a three-part question. Together, as a family, we dug amazing truths out of the text—and no one in our family would say this was either dull or painful.

This method requires that everyone think through what the passage is saying. Ideas go through the thought processes and come out of the mouth. We experience a great thing: the joy of discovery. What is discovered for one's self is always more meaningful than what is told to us by someone else.

It is exciting to see how the use of this method can become ingrained in a child's thought pattern and how this can enable him to take apart a piece of literature and comprehend what it is really saying. Children learn to listen, to isolate key ideas, to contrast and compare, and to come up with the heart of the text with the delight of a scuba diver seeking a treasure on the ocean floor. Over the years and with a variety of ages, we have found the benefits for our family have gone far beyond what we envisaged when we began this simple plan for Bible reading.

We have tried to handle the Bible honestly, letting it say what it says, not overly spiritualizing facts (which I believe turns children off because it lacks integrity to make a sermon out of what isn't there). The Bible is superb literature. It carries its own truth if we dig out the facts and apply them. We don't have to force its contents.

No need to attempt to protect truth, to explain away seeming inconsistencies either. Truth will turn out to be truth. Sometimes we came up with questions we couldn't answer. We've tried to relate the Bible to everyday happenings, school studies, and new findings. When we've come upon words like fornication, circumcision, etc., we've talked openly about what these mean. If you have trouble explaining, look them up together in the dictionary. The Bible's teaching about morality and sex is still appropriate today.

No other tongue in the world has the advantage of so many modern translations of the Bible as English does! By all means, use contemporary English translations in your family Bible readings. The other day a woman said to me, "I like to stick with the original Bible." I didn't bother to tell her she would have to learn Greek and Hebrew to do that! The King James Version of the Bible was translated in 1611, and while its language flow is beautiful, particularly in the Psalms, young people deserve the privilege of hearing God speak their own language in a contemporary translation.

For those who are adventuresome, buy each member of your family an interlinear Greek New Testament to read together as your family matures. The English words appear above the Greek words, and one family we know has taught themselves the basics of Greek in this fashion.

All of us want the Bible to be a living Book for our children. One truth seems overwhelmingly obvious, however. No matter what technique we use, our own attitude is the key. We must be *genuine*. Our blatant inconsistencies linked with outward piety will battle the authority of the Bible in our children's lives.

If we approach the Bible with a stained-glass window voice and emotional tremors that make the book seem "religious," in the most frightening sense of that word, chances are our children will escape at the first opportunity. Our prayers, too, must reflect that we are speaking with Someone who is real, not that we are making a speech and using prayer as a way to scold someone.

The kind of family Bible reading I have been discussing is no rigid ritual that makes rules more important than people. On the contrary, it is because people—people God has given to us—are *so very* important that we are compelled to personal discipline in this matter. When we, as families, treat the Bible as our necessary food, obviously respecting its authority by our own personal obedience, our children will find in this Book what they will never find in any other way: the way of eternal life—without which there can be no lasting enjoyment of God's gifts.

I have talked about many books in the preceding pages, books that will enrich a child's life. If you think my emphasis has been imbalanced—that I have put other books ahead of the Bible—you are mistaken. For at least eighteen years a child lives in our home. If we read the Bible as a regular habit, what conclusion will that child draw from our emphasis?

You will determine your child's attitude toward the Book and books by the paths you open up for him. And it will affect your children's children and the free, imaginative communication of the Good News in the years to come.

Illustration by Satomi Ichikawa from GRANDPA'S SOUP by Eiko Kadono.
Used by permission Eerdmans Books. © 1997

Chapter 8

Who Influences Your Children?

About 390 B.C. Socrates wrote about Athenian society:

> Could I climb the highest place in Athens, I would lift up my voice and proclaim, "Fellow citizens, why do you burn and scrape every stone to gather wealth, and take so little care of your children to whom you must one day relinquish all?"

Concern for the well-being of children and quality family life is not new! People must repeatedly be reminded that societies do not disintegrate; families do. And when family life fails, individuals experience a deep loneliness and disorientation. They look for someone to belong to and grope for some idea worth believing in.

Home: A Safe Place

No matter how sophisticated or laid-back our society becomes, the word *home* remains one of the most emotionally evocative words in the English language. *Home* is where a person belongs. It seems to be a place of universal longing.

What is *home?* My favorite definition is "a safe place," a place where one is free from attack, a place where one experiences secure relationships and affirmation. It's a place where people share and understand each other. Its relationships are nurturing. The people in it do not

*Home is
a safe place.*

need to be perfect; instead, they need to be honest, loving, supportive, recognizing a common humanity that makes all of us vulnerable.

A home of people who claim to belong to God has an extra plus: God at the center. All our inadequacies and fears are under his lordship; our strengths and excitements are placed under his control. His love inspires ours; his forgiveness is the basis of our forgiveness of one another; his instructions are our guide. The claim to be Christian is not an easy boast. We have repeatedly made the word *Christian* into an adjective when it is meant to be a noun: a person who follows Christ.

This affirmation of persons is no small thing. It is the heart of life. All persons need to know and believe in their value and need to have the self-esteem that comes with that deep inner assurance. Most profoundly we find our worth in the heart of God and in his love for us. But many people have difficulty believing God really loves them when they have been cheated from basic acceptance in their families. Tragically, some people spend most of their lives trying to prove their personal worth, trying to feel good about themselves. Their relationships suffer at every level because their self needs are so absorbing.

Virginia Satir, a family therapist, in her book *People-making*, makes a decisive statement, based on her years of observation of family life:

> In all troubled families I noticed that self-worth was low; communication was indirect, vague, and not really honest; rules were rigid, inhuman, non-negotiable, and everlasting; and the link to society was fearful, placating, and blaming.
>
> In vital and nurturing families I consistently see a different pattern. Self-worth is high; communication is direct, clear, specific, and honest; rules are flexible, human, appropriate, and subject to change; and the linking to society is open and hopeful.[1]

Her observation makes sense to me: a good view of self, open communication, flexibility and understanding, and a hopeful, positive link to the world around us. It is my contention that reading good books together and talking about them is basic to experiencing this kind of family life.

Our Personal Influence

This brings into focus our personal influence within our homes, and the spotlight settles on individual parents. Parents need basic self-esteem, for they set the pattern. Our influence flows out of our selves, our values, our priorities, and our basic understanding of the meaning

[1]Virginia Satir, *People-making* (Palo Alto, Calif.: Science and Behavior Books, Inc., 1972), p. 4.

of life. Parents need to make decisions to *be* as well as to *do*. What we are affects others significantly. Husbands and wives who affirm each other will be those who best affirm their children. Affirming, nurturing people influence others far beyond their intention simply because they provide rich soil in which individual personalities can grow.

Similarly, those parents who have carefully examined their values and their view of life are going to be those parents whose influence on their children is most consistent. Why? Because what they believe is important to them. Believing something is true means eliminating things that are not. Our priorities are determined by our values.

Communication flows out of conviction. Far too many parents feel little responsibility beyond providing physical needs, seeing that order is kept, and making sure that their children are at the right places at the right time. They do not plan to be influencers of ideas, to furnish the mind with what is true. They expect the school and the church to do that for them.

On the other hand, some authoritarian parents believe that the word *influence* means propagandizing or dominating the spirit of another. You cannot bully people into appreciating what is true and good and beautiful. Out of sheer necessity to retain individual personhood, the independent spirit in a child will reject the parent whose message is "only my way to do it."

Influence does not mean overwhelming another person. Instead, it is being sure enough of what is true and good to have our actions (lifestyle) and our words affect someone else. A word study here is interesting. The root meaning of *influence* has a sense of "flowing into," but in common usage it has come to mean "the exertion of action of which the operation is unseen, except in its effect."

We influence by what we are and by what we do. In one sense, it could be said that we influence others simply by being. We can all think of the colorless, inept teacher who did little to affect our lives, in contrast to the convinced, dedicated teacher who had personal goals and standards for us as students that we didn't always like.

Our Changing Society

Margaret Mead, in her book *Culture and Commitment*, wrote about three kinds of societal patterns in American history. In the first, called *postfigurative*, the line of influence passes relatively unhindered from the grandfather to the father to the son. The grandfather expects the son's values to be the same as his own, even though he does not verbalize them. They work together, having limited contact with others outside the family, and in the constancy of each other's company the influence is effective. Perhaps this is best seen in pioneer America or in television programs like *The Waltons* or in stories like *Little House on the Prairie*—and may even still exist in some tightly knit ethnic groups.

The second pattern Mead calls *cofigurative*. With the industrial revolution, the move to cities, and the consolidated school, children came under new influence from their peers. The voice of peers subdued the voice of parental influence. Stimulating one another, the young did what their peers did and adopted habits and styles that caused parents to wring their hands. Peer pressure was a force to be reckoned with.

The third pattern, called *prefigurative*, is a society with thousands of voices crying out to be heard, with messages to be received. Media pressure is added to peer pressure. Communication experts say that the average person sees about 800 to 1200 advertisements a day as he or she turns the pages in magazines and newspapers, passes billboards, and hears commercials—even though these messages may not be consciously perceived. Add to this the onslaught of television programming with its varied propaganda regarding lifestyles, the news, as well as those "good" programs we approve, and you have a massive invasion of ideas into the head of a young person.

Margaret Mead projected even greater changes for the future and even stronger influences. She concluded that no one has ever lived in this kind of technological world before. Therefore, she concluded, we cannot teach children what is valuable because we don't know what is valuable for this kind of world; we can only teach them the value of commitment.

At this point Margaret Mead and I part company (if, indeed, we ever were in company), because I believe we do know what values are unchanging in a changing world. And we can and must teach them to our children, or they will have trouble extracting them from the babble of our noisy environment.

My great concern is that parents are living in a prefigurative world (to use Miss Mead's coinage) as though it were postfigurative. We must do more than live in the same house with our children. We need to spend time with them, talk to them, share our lives with them, and teach them. The words of God to the parents of Israel are so significant I must repeat them again: "Love the LORD your God with all your heart and with all your soul and with all your strength. These commandments that I give you today are to be upon your hearts. Impress them on your children. Talk about them when you sit at home and when you walk along the road, when you lie down and when you get up" (Deuteronomy 6:5–7). Influencing our children is not a casual task. It won't get done unless we have a plan.

The Influence of Television

We can hardly dismiss the influence of television with a shrug. This media shapes our children's points of view and affects them emotionally, intellectually, and spiritually. Sociologists and psychologists conclude that anti-personal-relation values, anti-cooperation values, and anti-democratic values are communicated by television programming. In one hour the viewer may see more adventure, more violence, and more excitement than the average person experiences in a lifetime. People become spectators, detached from their own lives, almost refusing to take responsibility for living.

Parents and teachers report greater tension, anxiety, restlessness, and suspicion in children after prolonged television viewing. Children thrive on noise and confusion, and even strife. Short attention spans are almost inevitably the result of preschool television programming that features an interruption every minute and a half. Children grow up seeing people break the law and beat the system on television. School authorities seem to believe this has lessened respect for all adult authority. Television often promotes hostility that children can't define, but they are then inclined to settle things with violence.

Personally, I have a strong negative reaction to Saturday morning television programs that congratulate children for having a day free from school in a way that implies an escape from prison or an otherwise miserable experience. Geared to electronic sound and fury, children may feel that books and even conversations are rather dull unless they are helped to see otherwise.

Without question television consumes the largest part of the average American's free time. It is estimated that by age sixty-five most Americans have spent *nine years of twenty-four-hour days* in front of the television set. By the time a typical American boy or girl has reached the age of eighteen, he or she has totaled 12,000 to 15,000 hours of television watching. These are not hours stolen from school, but from relating to other people. It is not surprising that so many young people want to drop out of life. They don't know how to live it. Increasingly we observe that university students do not know how to relate well to other human beings.

> *Influencing our children is not a casual task. It won't get done unless we have a plan.*

The most serious problem with television is not its programs (although that is a subject worth discussion), but its destruction of the average family's exchange of views and information at the evening meal. People are anxious to get to a favorite program, and so they hurry to finish eating. What happened during the day, little ideas or larger matters, are never discussed. Further, statistics indicate that many families eat no more than three meals together a week. When does a family talk together?

When I hear university students say, "There's only so much time a person can spend with his parents," then I usually assume they aren't used to talking together as a family, sharing their lives, feeling together, or exchanging ideas. It is like saying there is only so much time one can spend with people. Parents are people, but some of them have never let their children know this. You can't wait to begin when they are grown up. You begin talking and sharing and listening when they are little.

My words on television and culture are not new to you as parents. You've heard all this many times. The question needs to be asked: What steps are you taking to change the pattern for your family? The truth about raising children is that you only go around once. You don't get a second chance. This is it!

An Unburdened Lifestyle

We are inclined to make life heavy and see only what *must* be done, not what *could* be done. As more and more mothers join the work force outside the home, this burdened way of life will increase. As William Wordsworth observed in "The World Is Too Much With Us":

> The world is too much with us; late and soon,
> Getting and spending, we lay waste our powers:
> Little we see in Nature that is ours;
> We have given our hearts away, a sordid boon!

We let the evening news take away our delight in the beauty of a sunset. The ugly becomes more real than the good. I think of G. K. Chesterton, who once remarked, "God may be younger than we are." God may say, "Let's have another sunrise." He delights in what he has made and is eternally creative. God is not weighed down by the disorder man has brought to the world, wringing his hands as if life were out of control. Sometimes we take on burdens that belong to God.

Maybe the worse thing in the world is to believe that today is exactly like yesterday. Then we forget to notice and to share what is new and fresh and good about today.

What is worse, as we grow older, we have difficulty stretching our minds to connect what may be small, delightful, and everyday with what is big, eternal, and true. That's what children (and children's literature) can do for us. That's why talking and sharing are so important for grown-ups, not just for children. C. S. Lewis spoke of a child who on Easter morning was heard whispering to himself, "Chocolate eggs and Jesus risen!" We need both the joy of chocolate eggs and Jesus risen in our lives.

Without this joy we become spectators of life, not feeling much, not expecting much, and always playing it safe. Truth and joy become the security of bank accounts instead of a sunrise or a bird's nest or a beautiful story.

Underlying all of this discussion is my thesis that parents who read widely together with their children are going to be those who most influence their children, who have the largest worldview, who have an uncommon delight in what is good and true and beautiful—and an uncommon commitment to it. Sharing and feeling and talking together will come naturally. Books shared with each other provide that kind of climate.

I can't prove it on a national scale, perhaps, but I'm a pretty convinced mother. When one of your children returns home from the university for summer vacation with two of his textbooks and says to his father, "I want to sell these, but before I do, I thought you would enjoy reading the pages I've marked in them," then you know that sharing books is a two-way street.

When your offspring shares his tense moments with you and comments, "Remember that story we read last summer—*That Hideous Strength* by C. S. Lewis? I found myself in a situation this week in which I felt all the pressures that book talks about—pressure to conform to the group and compromise my values to be part of the inner-ring. Suddenly that story came back to me and I remembered what an awful mistake it is to play the game that way"—then you have courage to boldly say to others that good books can influence behavior.

And when your husband finishes reading James Thurber's *The White Deer* aloud to you in bed one night, sighs, and says, "Let's send it immediately for our married children to share," then you know that together you've set in motion a lifelong pattern that makes for rich living.

Parents who read widely together with their children are going to be those who most influence their children.

A frog came along and sat down beside me.

"Nice boat," he said.

Chapter 9

Making Decisions about Books

By now you have gathered that I am pretty convinced about the wonderful gifts reading brings to the life of a child. I hope you have caught my sense of awe about your opportunities as a parent to write on the pages of your child's life. Every parent by words and choices furnishes the heart and mind of a child, for good or for ill. I am lobbying for intentional use of words and books to influence a child in the best possible way. What do books bring a child? A recap is in order: a big world with all its possibilities—people to know and understand, places to imagine, eyes to see beyond the obvious, words to stretch the mind and heart, and a lasting stewardship of language used in the right way.

Using Words to Nurture Your Children

Language is an instrument; it is even more an environment. We create a climate with words. God spoke and created a world. On a different level, we also speak and create a world for our children.

Our words will be important to the children in our homes from the day they are born. And probably even before that. After I had successfully quieted our newborn grandson, I remarked to his mother that he seemed to like it when I sang to him. She affirmed this and

Plan a regular read-aloud time with your child.

said, "He's used to it. I've been singing to him for months before I knew who he would be!"

Before children are more than a week old they can distinguish one voice from another, and within a few months they respond with their own jargon. Talking and singing or reciting nursery rhymes provides a warm atmosphere in which to grow. Babies ought not to be bathed, dressed, or tucked into bed in silence. Your own spontaneous conversation with them encourages them to respond with their own. They get used to the rhythm and joy of words. Nursery rhymes are a natural for this seeming one-sided dialogue in which you indulge yourself. The details of living bring to mind *Rub-a-dub-dub; One, two, buckle my shoe; Rock-a-bye baby; Rain, rain, go away; Polly put the kettle on; Higgledy, piggledy, my black hen; Patti-cake.* I have a hunch Moses' mother sang such rhymes to him as she tucked him in his basket.

These "conversations" are important to children. I'm sure many three-year-olds keep asking *Why?* not so much out of intellectual curiosity as out of a desire to keep you talking. They feel good about conversation. You'll hear a child talk to his stuffed animals much the way you talk to him. If you talk down to him, he'll talk down to his animals. If you use baby talk, so will he. If your conversation helps him notice his environment, then you will hear him comment in this way in his monologues. You are building his vocabulary and enlarging his awareness by treating him as a person in your conversations. Remember: *A person's a person no matter how small.*

That's how we begin, and although we're not consciously thinking about books when we hold these loving conversations with the young, we are getting a child ready to read. Words are important. Picture books that tell a story will follow naturally, and sooner than you realize a child will begin to "read" the pictures and make up his own story. *Do You Want to Be My Friend?* by Eric Carle is a favorite book without many words. It begins with a small gray mouse asking the questions that lead the reader through the pages. *A Boy, A Dog, A Frog, A Friend* by Mercer Mayer can be "read" by children as young as two.

Plan a regular read-aloud time with your child. Few activities are as rewarding as this in creating a warm relationship. There is a good feeling in sharing a story at any age. The reading list at the back of this book begins with books to be read to the very young. Children who are read to from the very first come to expect that a book brings pleasure, that letters make words, that words put together in the right way say something that is fun.

Building Your Child's Library

At two years old children usually become possessive. This is the time to have a few books that are "my very own." Even the size and shape will be important. Favorites will be looked at hundreds of times and greeted as old friends. As children grow older, they will want more. A few well-chosen books personally owned can give a child a sense of value, companionship, and individuality—more valuable than fifty volumes hastily read and returned to the library. A person does need to own some books—choice volumes that become part of one's life— but how do you decide which books to buy?

Give books as gifts, but be prepared to pay the price for them. Resist the cheap books found on grocery store racks designed to encourage impulse buying. These aren't quality stories for the most part (if you read them aloud, you'll realize this) and make no lasting contribution to a library. There is another price to pay sometimes. People, including children, have gotten used to flat packages from me, but I am reminded of the little boy next door who was hoping for a toy at age four, but when he opened my package he exclaimed, "A book—and I can't even read!" No matter; he grew up to be a book-loving young man.

On the other hand, our sixteen-year-old nephew wrote us a thank-you letter for a gift, our latest contribution to his library (the C. S. Lewis science-fiction trilogy), and in his own inimitable way expressed appreciation for every addition we'd made to his library from the very first. He put an asterisk next to that sentence and footnoted at the bottom of the page: *Age three:* A Hole Is to Dig, *and I still remember you reading it to me.* A good book makes a lasting impression! Can you imagine him commenting on a gift of clothing or a toy thirteen years later?

Of course you will begin with a good nursery rhyme book by a good illustrator. Don't get a flimsy, common one. Buy one that is really beautiful, one the child will want to pass on to his or her children!

A child needs some picture books that say "good night" or talk about the child's world in a way that gives feelings of safety and love. Be sure to include at least one good poetry book (and buy a new one for each major shift in comprehension) and read it aloud. Next you'll add a few storybooks like *Little Toot* by Hardie Gramatky or *Make Way for Ducklings* by Robert McCloskey or Marjorie Flack's *Ask Mr. Bear* or *Mike Mulligan and His Steam Shovel* by Virginia Burton, already loved for over sixty years.

Lyle was always one for sharing.

From *Lyle, Lyle, Crocodile* by Bernard Waber. Copyright © 1965.
Reproduced by permission of Houghton Mifflin Company.

When you take this book with you to the bookstore, its book list will help you find what you want. Look the books over carefully. You won't be able to buy them all, and some will obviously appeal to you more than others. You will know what is just right for the child you have in mind. Trust your judgment.

Children love animal books: *Bread and Jam for Frances* by Russell Hoban; *Lyle, Lyle Crocodile* by Bernard Waber; *George and Martha* by James Marshall; *Corduroy* by Don Freeman and many others fit in this category.

Softcover editions put many of these good books within reach of our pocketbooks. Children's hardcover books are often unusually expensive, largely because of the colored illustrations. The new paperbacks mean that every child can own more books. The good paperbacks are printed from the same plates as the original hardcover editions. Children like paperbacks and often choose them over hardcover editions because they are soft and more flexible. As one child remarked, "This book seems more friendly."

However, the binding will not last as long on a paperback, and you will want certain special books in hardcover. One of these is the classic *The Wind in the Willows*. I'm especially fond of Scribner's anniversary edition with illustrations by Ernest Shepard. We read this aloud in our family at about age eight. Later at age eighteen it was pulled off the shelf again with the comment, "I'd forgotten how really good this book is!" Worth reading at age eight and worth reading at eighteen.

How can you tell which ones to buy in hardcover? The answer may vary with your family tastes. Part of the answer is in the lasting quality of the story. I think A. A. Milne's original *Winnie-the-Pooh* is worth hardcover; C. S. Lewis's Narnia Chronicles and Lewis Carroll's *Alice in Wonderland* and others like this have stood the test of time. But such choices also reflect our family tastes. Yours may be different.

You have already discovered that the books children love will be read over and over and over—regardless of whether in hardcover or softcover. Many parents can recite Margaret Wise Brown's *Good Night Moon* by heart. Generations of children have loved it, and it is now available in a board book that is almost indestructible, just right for small hands and even withstands some exploration by new teeth.

As they grow older, let children help you choose books and discuss with them why you don't buy some books on impulse, even if all you say is, "Let's buy a really good book." You are helping decide on quality. Treating books carefully and returning them to the special place where books are kept is an important part of owning a library.

Many families set aside money to buy at least one book a month. It should be a family project. Sometimes your children may decide to buy a book they have already read from the library because the experience in reading it was so fine that they want to own it. That is like choosing an old friend to be with you forever.

If you are isolated from a bookstore that carries a large selection of children's books, use the library to decide what you want and then order it by mail or online. Schools have wonderful book sales. Over the years Scholastic Books has provided good selections of books at good prices. The children's librarian will also be able to furnish you with sources.

As independence and reading interest grow, take your child with you to the book fairs where secondhand books are sold. Both of you must be able to recognize authors and the books you would really want to own to make this profitable. I have known children to find beautifully bound editions of *Moby Dick, Tom Sawyer,* or *Treasure Island* on such excursions.

One book is a must: a dictionary—a good dictionary with large enough print to invite reading. If you can afford it, *The Random House Dictionary* is first-rate and goes beyond an ordinary dictionary to include some details found in an encyclopedia. It's a big book and must be kept accessible.

Make "looking it up" a family habit. We keep a dictionary near our dinner table so that in the course of discussion it is easy to verify meanings and learn new things. It doesn't have to be a big dictionary. *Webster's Collegiate Dictionary* will do as well. Every home should have one handy. Dictionaries make wonderful graduation gifts for a personal library later on.

Our family values a good atlas as part of a standard family library. We have the *National Geographic World Atlas*, which allows us a careful look at the far places of the world. The evening news becomes more meaningful, as well as places mentioned in the books we read.

Using the Library

You will want your child to enjoy far more books than you can buy. This means regular trips to the library. Almost all libraries have extensive children's sections, and a library card becomes an important possession. Begin visiting the library together at an early age, and allow plenty of time to look and choose.

Notice authors and illustrators, and call your child's attention to them. That's the first step in beginning to find your way in a library. A child who feels at home in a library at a young age will be one who uses the library all life long. Once you enter the world of children's literature, your eye will catch book reviews in magazines and newspapers, and soon you will feel quite at home exploring and discovering authors you like.

Don't be afraid to check out a large stack of books—as many as the library allows. You will make some good selections, while some will be less appealing when you get them home. That's how you learn what to look for and help your children learn as well. You haven't lost anything if your choice turns out to be disappointing. You aren't committed to read it, and next time you will be wiser.

The Difference in Children

Not all children take to books like ducks to puddles. Each child is a special person. Some are just poor readers or lack motivation. We may take it for granted, but learning to read is an amazing feat. Someone said it was as magical as rubbing two sticks together and creating a fire.

Dyslexia causes complications and needs special attention from aware parents who should take advantage of the many resources to help overcome this problem. For others reading is difficult for different reasons. Parents can make a game out of the letter-sounds, perhaps using the refrigerator to list words that begin with the "B" sound or the "C" sound or whatever. Post labels on familiar things around the house to help with letter recognition. Make learning to read an adventure, and don't take the skills of those who do it easily for granted. Children do have original ideas. One of the boys in our family had trouble conceding that the letters of the alphabet had to be in a certain order for a reason. He was reluctant to abandon his way of reciting the alphabet with his own creative arrangement, different each time.

This is when family togetherness in books comes to the rescue, at least in part. Reading aloud and sharing a book demonstrates that stories are fun, that books are friends regardless of reading skills. Getting children reading on their own might mean a careful curtailing of easier substitutes, but a parent in cooperation with a creative God ought to be able to come up with other assists. Try reading aloud an exciting story with such a child—a story one couldn't bear to leave uncompleted—and then push the child to finish it on his own. Make certain the project doesn't lead to failure because it is too difficult, and be available for help. Whetting a child's appetite this way and then helping to find another book by the same author could mean a fresh start for the child. But it takes a sensitive parent who cares. I am convinced that many poor readers have developed psychological blocks early in their reading career, often by comparing themselves with rapid readers who leave them behind in the dust.

Don't put a premium on speed, and never say, "That book is much too young for you!" If a child can read it, encourage the reading. Let the child read it over and over. Coax children onward without threatening their self-image in the complicated joy of reading.

I read *The Puddle* by David McPhail to a small boy recently. It's the story of a rainy day and a boy who puts on his boots and raingear with permission to sail his boat in a puddle. Soon a frog hops into the scene, commenting, "Nice boat" and sails away on the boat, ignoring the boy's call, "Come back!" An alligator arrives to help rescue the boat before it sails out of sight; later a pig joins the group and takes a swim in the puddle before an elephant arrives and drinks the puddle dry. What an adventure! Later, when he arrives home, the boy is content

Reading aloud and sharing a book demonstrates that stories are fun, that books are friends regardless of reading skills.

to be put into the bathtub by his mother, where he again happily sails his boat. The ridiculous in the story, the unusual animal appearances, and then the felt-safety of a boy sailing his boat in his own bathtub—it was both adventurous and cozy as the small boy and I sat close together, sharing. After a sigh and a pause, the small boy said, "Let's read it again!" It's an experience hard to beat.

Part 2

Best-Loved Books for Children

*Books Your Children Should
Have the Opportunity to Enjoy*

GOD also sent them flocks of birds called quails, which they cooked and ate.

Illustration by Brian Wildsmith from EXODUS by Brian Wildsmith.
Used by permission of Eerdmans Books. © 1998

Chapter 10

How to Use the Book List

Childhood is brief, and without some guidance a child may miss what is quality reading and never discover the pleasure of a well-written book. It seems wisest to pack all the goodness we can into the formative years. That's why book lists are helpful.

A book list is as good as the understanding of the person who compiled it. Book lists for preschoolers through grades three are generally in agreement. Lists for older readers may sometimes reflect the compiler's view of what it means to be contemporary or relevant.

I've tried to avoid all questionable reading in my bibliography and to include primarily those books that would both delight and benefit children. Not every good book is included. You may ask, "Why did she leave this one out?" I may have missed it, or it was simply left out in the process of selection. It's too much to think I could include everything, but I have tried to list those books that will still be considered superior reading years from now.

Listing books according to age is risky because maturity and reading levels vary so much. If your children are good readers, don't let them miss the good books that are just right for their particular age in your eagerness to see how advanced they are in reading!

Take Time to Get Acquainted with Books

A book list can help you browse the library or the bookstore. For example, if you are interested in purchasing a Mother Goose book, compare the various editions and choose one that pleases you most.

The annotations in my book list are of necessity very brief. Each book deserves far more enthusiastic comment than I've included, but it is hard to do justice to plot and characters in two sentences.

Various medals and awards are given each year by several societies for the best books published. Two of the most familiar are the Caldecott Medal and the Newbery Award. The Caldecott (CM in our list), awarded annually since 1938 to the artist of the most distinguished picture book for children, is named for Ralph Caldecott, the famous illustrator of books for children. Caldecott Honor (CH in our list) books are also noted. The Newbery Medal (NM in our list), named after John Newbery, has been awarded annually since 1921 to the author of the most distinguished contribution to American literature for children during the preceding year. With the output of so many good books, it is hard to choose only one, so others are listed as Newbery Honor (NH) books. The Boston Globe/Horn Book award (BG/HB) has a prestigious group of judges that help highlight exceptional books. Noteworthy books written by and about African-Americans are awarded the Coretta Scott King award (CSK), a fairly recent addition to the award lists. New award categories keep appearing each year, in an attempt to keep good books in the public eye. Don't let a medal or an award dictate your reading, however. Some books may miss the judges' eyes and become your favorites. The awarding task is formidable in the face of so many good books.

As you take your children to the library or bookstore and begin noticing books, you will be surprised at how aware you become of what is good, better, and best. This world of children's books is a splendid one to explore and enjoy. And you will have a new appreciation for the wonder of words.

Remember that reading abilities and interests differ. Many teens enjoy books listed here in the 9–12 age category (so do I and many other adults). It's best not to say, "This book is too young for you!" The story may be memorable for any age. Many adults love children's picture books like *Olivia* or *The Gardener* or *The Rooster's Gift* and others as much as children do. Read widely. A good book is a good book!

Simple and Profound

Picture books at the outset seem simple, but the good ones say important things that will furnish your children with good concepts, ideas to talk about and think through, ideas to stick in a child's mind for years to come. Don't dismiss them too quickly, especially for ages six through eight. Develop a mind-set that thinks from the child's point of view. Often a book will tug at your own heart, giving you new insights and even a new direction for you and your children to explore.

In a hurry to grow up, some children (and their parents) skip books that could influence their character profoundly. I think of one precocious seven-year-old, so self-absorbed that she has few friends, whose mother reads books aloud that are aimed at twelve-year-olds and skips the ones for children that spell out kindness and caring like *A Chair for Mother* by Vera Williams or Patricia Polacco's *Chicken Sunday*, or many others that offer simple, but good ideas about living. To miss books like these is to miss part of what books offer a family.

When I read Mem Fox's *Wilfrid Gordon McDonald Partridge*, with Julie Vivas' lively illustrations, I felt the impact of this book on my own life. It's the story of a little boy who lives next to a retirement home where he becomes friends with the old folks who live there through his daily visits. From threads in this wonderful story, I saw new possibilities of taking children on regular visits to such centers to let the magic of young children do its work in the lives of the elderly. Simple can be profound.

Often a book will tug at your own heart, giving you new insights.

Now Find the "Honey" for Yourself

Preparing this book list has been a delightful exercise—exploring the new books that have been published since the last edition of *Honey for a Child's Heart* and making sure to include the classics that never go out of print. The luxury of having so many imaginative, thoughtful, humorous, and enriching books available at the library and in bookstores is something to appreciate.

To make it easier for you to find the books you want, look for the following arrangement:

- I have divided the book list into chapters by age of the reader.
- Within each chapter the books are listed alphabetically by author.

- Two chapters list special books considered long-standing classics: chapter 12 (picture book classics) and chapter 15 (classic children's novels).

The rest of the listing is obvious. Check the table of contents for specifics.

I hope as you peruse my book list that new windows will be opened for you. I could wish you nothing better than that you become a joyful dispenser of "honey" to those you love and feel richer for having done so. Happy reading!

Chapter 11

A Child's First Books: Ages 0–3

When parents ask me when to begin reading to a child, I always say, "Right away!" But, of course, I am not talking about reading to infants who can't focus their eyes. Newborns need gentle rocking and lullabies more than books; they are still learning to look at their parents.

But within a few months the world around infants comes into focus—worth noticing and exploring through books. What a great idea to give infant "readers" the relatively new and popular board books! First of all, board books are pretty indestructible. They even survive new teeth, and that's a wonder in itself. More than that, they are just the right size for small hands. The pages turn easily and even unintentionally as muscle control develops. Suddenly a new image to look at appears as the child plays with the book.

The best board books and beginner picture books are those first written with infants and toddlers in mind, books like *Runaway Bunny* or *Have You Seen My Duckling?* Some publishers are diluting classic stories from the past and making them into board books, and you will want to be aware of this when choosing books. Looking to extend a product, these publishers take the characters from a well-loved story for older children and simplify the story to fit a younger audience. I mention this, not because I think these books will scar your child's psyche, but because you need to decide if you want to trivialize great stories in this way. Even Pooh loses out with too early an exposure.

Board books are only part of the treasures awaiting toddlers. Illustrators have produced magical books for little people, both in hardcover and softcover. A child's first books introduce wonderful colors, new things to notice, and the assuring cadence of select words to make the world both hopeful and wonderful.

Here are some good books for your little ones.

Board Books

Margaret Wise Brown, *Big Red Barn,* il. Felicia Bond.
_____, *Good Night, Moon,* il. Clement Hurd.
> A forever favorite bedtime book.

_____, *Runaway Bunny,* il. Clement Hurd.
> Cuddly assurance of love.

Eric Carle, *The Very Hungry Caterpillar.*
> He eats a hole right through the book!

_____, *The Very Busy Spider.*
_____, *Have You Seen My Cat?*
_____, *Will You Be My Friend?*
> All of Carle's books have a winsome charm.

Tomie dePaola, *Tomie's Little Mother Goose.*
> A wonderful first introduction to Mother Goose.

Mem Fox, *Time for Bed,* il. Jane Dyer.
> A favorite sleepy-time story.

John Graham, *I Love You, Mouse,* il. Tomie dePaola.
> A sweet book about caring for whoever you love.

Eric Hill, *Where's Spot.*

Nina Laden, *Peek-a-Who.*
> Who will you find hiding?

Iona Archibald Opie, *Humpty-Dumpty and Other Rhymes,*
> il. Rosemary Wells.
> Another delightful Mother Goose book.

Al Perkins, *Hand, Hand, Finger, Thumb,* il. Eric Gurney.
> A rhythm book little children love.

Peggy Rathmann, *Good Night, Gorilla.*

Constance Robinson, *My First Truck Board Book.*

Feodor Rojankovsky, *The Great Big Wild Animal Book.*
> A silly, silly book for sleepy children.

Jerry Smith, *The Wheels on the Bus,* il. Jerry Smath.
> A popular children's song is brought to life.

Dr. Seuss, *Mr. Brown Can Moo, Can You: Dr. Seuss's Book
of Wonderful Noises.*

Ring-o ring o'roses.

From *Book of Nursery and Mother Goose Rhymes* by Marguerite de
Angeli. Copyright © 1953, 1954 by Marguerite de Angeli. Reprinted
by permission of Doubleday & Company, Inc.

BG/HB	Boston Globe/Horn Book award
CM	Caldecott Medal
CH	Caldecott Honor
CSK	Coretta Scott King award
NA	Newbery Award
NH	Newbery Honor
NM	Newbery Medal

Peter Spier, *Big Trucks, Little Trucks.*
_____, *Fast Cars, Slow Cars.*
_____, *Here Come the Fire Trucks.*
_____, *Trucks That Dig and Dump.*
> Four wonderful board books by a favorite illustrator.

Brian Wildsmith, *Animal Seasons.*
_____, *Animal Colors.*
_____, *ABC.*

Vera Williams, *More More More Said the Baby: 3 Love Stories.* CH

Toddler Picture Books

Graeme Base, *Animalia.*

Marc T. Brown, *Hand Rhymes.*
> Put your hands up and prepare to wiggle through fourteen games of hand movements.

Lois Ehlert, *Color Zoo.* CH
> Fascinating use of colors and cutouts to learn animals and shapes.

_____, *Market Day.*
> Ehlert's ingredients from different cultures make going to market delicious.

_____, *Color Farm.*
_____, *Nuts to You.*
_____, *Eating the Alphabet: Fruits and Vegetables from A to Z.*

Denise Fleming, *In the Small, Small Pond.* CH
> Who lives in the pond? Fleming's unique art form gives movement to images and words.

_____, *The Everything Book.*
_____, *In the Tall, Tall Grass.*
_____, *Where Once There Was a Wood.*
_____, *Time to Sleep.*

Stephen T. Johnson, *Alphabet City.*
_____, *City by Numbers.*

Ann Jonas, *Color Dance.*

Tan Koide, *May We Sleep Here Tonight?* il. Yasuko Koide.

> Back in print after fifteen years of neglect, this is a classic bedtime story.

Bill Martin Jr. and John Archambault, *Chicka Chicka Boom Boom,* il. Lois Ehlert.

Sam McBratney, *Guess How Much I Love You,* il. Anita Jeram.

> A soothing tale of love that Little Nutbrown Hare thinks can be measured.

Shirley Neitzel, *The Dress I'll Wear to the Party,* il. Nancy Winslow Parker.

> It's dress-up time and every kid enjoys it.

_____, *The Jacket I Wear in the Snow.*
_____, *The Bag I'm Taking to Grandma's.*

Anne Rockwell, *Things That Go.*

> Take a trip to the sea, city, park, or just stay at home and note what "goes" there.

_____, *What We Like.*

Janet Morgan Stoeke, *A Hat for Minerva Louise.*

> An odd chicken (who loves snow) hunts for the perfect hat to wear.

_____, *Minerva Louise.*
_____, *Minerva Louise at School.*
_____, *Minerva Louise at the Fair.*

Stephen R. Swinburne, *What's Opposite?*

Nancy Tafuri, *Have You Seen My Duckling?* CM

> Each page has a hidden duckling to discover.

_____, *I Love You, Little One.*

> A bedtime assurance of being loved.

_____, *Silly Little Goose.*

> She keeps building her nest in another animal's domain.

Mother Goose:

Choose one for your permanent library from the many in print with a variety of illustrators. Four bestsellers are:

Sylvia Long's Mother Goose.

The Real Mother Goose, il. Blanche Fisher Wright.

> Now in an eightieth anniversary edition!

Mother Goose: The Original Volland Edition, il. Frederick Richardson.

> First published in 1915.

Mother Goose. Edited by Willy Pogany and published in 1928.

Ellen Stoll Walsh, *Mouse Magic,* il. Diane D'Andrade.

It's as if the colors are dancing on the paper as mouse finds out what happens when you mix colors.

Sue Williams, *I Went Walking,* il. Julie Vivas.

A stroll through the farm, seeing all the animals "looking at me."

_____, *Let's Go Visiting.*

Chapter 12

Picture Book Classics: Ages 4–8

The story-telling artists listed here are legendary. Most of these books have been in print for fifty years and some for nearly a hundred—classics to be sure! Any books these authors create are worthy reading and good additions to your child's library. Some of these illustrators appear in the board book lists, but board books are a relatively new product, and these authors appeared originally in hardcovers and then softcovers.

Perhaps the reason these author/illustrators hold such a special place in children's literature is that early editors, limited in the number of books they could publish, held to stringent standards, working closely and demandingly with book creators to refine their product. They dare not publish a questionable product; every book must be a winner! Children's literature had not yet come into the prominence it now has. The letters of the formidable Ursula Nordstrom (published in *Dear Genius*) record the family feeling that developed between editors and book creators, and the great attention paid to details.

I find it interesting that the notable Margaret Wise Brown, whose *Good Night Moon* has sold over five million copies since it was first published in 1947, died unexpectedly at the age of forty-two in 1952. Yet her books live on and continue to be published. In 1991, on a visit to Brown's sister in Vermont, a literary agent found a cache of unpublished manuscripts in an attic room. The result: dozens of new Brown books are now being published with pictures by outstanding contemporary illustrators, like David Diaz for *The Little Scarecrow Boy*. Meanwhile, books that have gone out of print are reappearing. Brown has a timeless style that attracts children.

I have placed these classics in a separate listing because they have set the standard for children's literature through the years. These are names and titles you should know about, and their books will tug at your hearts for years to come. These are collector's items—books you will pass on to your children's children and beyond. The age range on these books can be anywhere from three to eight—and maybe eighty.

Margaret Wise Brown, *Little Fur Family*, il. Garth Williams.
    A new edition of a classic book of rhymes about furry friends.
_____, *The Color Kitten*, il. Alice and Martin Provinson.
    A child's first book about colors.
_____, *The Important Book*, il. Leonard Weisgard.
    What is important about rain? That it is wet.
_____, *Two Little Trains*, il. Leo and Diane Dillon.
_____, *Mouse of My Heart: A Treasury of Sense and Nonsense*,
    il. Loretta Krupinski.
_____, *Wait Till the Moon Is Full*, il. Garth Williams.
_____, *Train to Timbuctoo*, il. Art Seiden.
_____, *The Little Scarecrow Boy*, il. David Diaz.

Virginia Burton, *Mike Mulligan and His Steam Shovel*.
    A race against time as Mike and his steam shovel dig a cellar.
    A long-loved book.
_____, *The Little House*. CM
    Story of a house in the country and the changes the years bring
    as the city moves closer.
_____, *Katy and the Big Snow*.
    A snow plow determines to save a small town in a blizzard.

Marjorie Flack, *Angus and the Cat*.
    Angus is a Scottish terrier who has some merry adventures
    with a cat.
_____, *The Story about Ping*.
    A little Chinese duck and his adventures on the Yangtze River.

_____, *Ask Mister Bear.*

> None of the animals can think of a suitable gift for a little boy's mother, so he asks Mr. Bear, who whispers a secret on the very last page!

Don Freeman, *Corduroy.*

> A teddy bear lives in a toy store and jumps off the shelf to go on a nighttime adventure to find a lost button.

_____, *A Pocket for Corduroy.*

_____, *Dandelion.*

> "Come as you are," the invitation read. But Dandelion decided to make himself over, and finds out it is best to be who you are.

_____, *Norman the Doorman.*

> Norman, a doormouse, is the hero in a Horatio Alger story of bravery and cleverness.

Paul Galdone, *Henny Penny.*

> One of many delightful and memorable old stories.

_____, *The Little Red Hen.*

_____, *Three Little Pigs.*

_____, *The Gingerbread Boy.*

_____, *Three Billy Goats Gruff.*

> Children have been enjoying Galdone's renditions for generations.

Hardie Gramatky, *Little Toot.*

> An old favorite. A mischievous little tugboat becomes a hero.

Ezra Jack Keats, *The Snowy Day.* CM

> A story of Peter's great fun in a snowy world. *The Snowy Day*, a 1963 Caldecott winner, is the first full-color book to feature a black hero, as do all of Ezra Jack Keats' subsequent books. Since Keats' death, publishers have hired illustrators to extend his work by creating new titles about Peter and Willie, in Keats' name. Look for the original Keats books!

_____, *Peter's Chair.*

> A gentle story about jealousy over a new family addition.

_____, *Whistle for Willie.*

> A boy longs to whistle so he can call his dog.

_____, *A Letter to Amy.*

> Peter worries about inviting a girl to his birthday party.

_____, *Goggles.*

BG/HB	Boston Globe/Horn Book award
CM	Caldecott Medal
CH	Caldecott Honor
CSK	Coretta Scott King award
NA	Newbery Award
NH	Newbery Honor
NM	Newbery Medal

Robert Kraus, *Whose Mouse Are You?* il. Jose Aruego.
>Catchy rhymes bursting with joyful ingenuity.

_____, *Herman the Helper.*

_____, *Milton the Early Riser.*

Ruth Krauss, *A Hole Is to Dig: A First Book of First Definitions,* il. Maurice Sendak.
>A collection of active definitions for preschoolers, such as "Hands are to hold" and "Dogs are for kissing people."

_____, *Open House for Butterflies*, il. Maurice Sendak.
>More definitions.

_____, *I'll Be You and You Be Me*, il. Maurice Sendak.
>A series of stories, poems, and kid-speak.

>Publishers are reissuing all the favorite Krauss/Sendak golden oldies.

Lois Lenski, *The Little Train.*

_____, *The Little Fire Engine.*

_____, *I Like Winter.*
>Wonderful books now back in print.

Mercer Mayer, *Just Me and My Dad.*

_____, *Just Me and My Little Brother.*
>Well-loved Critter books to warm the heart.

_____, *A Boy, A Dog, A Frog.*
>Part of a series for preschoolers.

_____, *There's a Nightmare in My Closet.*

_____, *There's Something in the Attic.*

_____, *There's an Alligator Under My Bed.*
>A humorous series to dispel fear.

Robert McCloskey, *Make Way for Ducklings.* CM
>What happens when Mother Duck brings up her family in the city of Boston.

_____, *Time of Wonder.*
>The joys of sailing on the sea.

_____, *One Morning in Maine.* CH
>Sal learns to accept her loss when her loose tooth falls out while she's clamming.

_____, *Blueberries for Sal.* CH
>Sal eats more blueberries than she picks.

Beatrix Potter, *The Tale of Peter Rabbit.*

> Plus twenty-two other volumes of miniature, beautifully illustrated books with characters like Jemina Puddle-Duck, Jeremy Fisher, Squirrel Nutkin, Benjamin Bunny, and others you should meet.

Hans A. Rey, *Curious George.*

> This small monkey has been finding trouble for over fifty years. Children identify with his curiosity.

Richard Scarry, *Best Word Book Ever.*
_____, *Early Bird.*

> All Scarry's books are full of detailed pictures toddlers love. There is so much to notice! Many are board books.

Jemima shares her troubles with the gentleman fox.

From *The Tale of Jemima Puddle-Duck*
by Beatrix Potter, copyright © Frederick Warne
& Co., Ltd. Used by permission.

Maurice Sendak, *Nutshell Library.*
> Four tiny books in a slipcase, full of fun and learning, and just the right size and flavor for little people.

_____, *Where the Wild Things Are.* CM
> Rebellious Max runs away from home to cavort with the wild things.

Uri Shulevitz, *Snow.* CH
> Waiting for it to snow can be hard!

_____, *The Treasure.*
> A gentle reminder of what treasures are.

_____, *Dawn.*
> A boy and his grandfather experience dawn on a camping trip.

_____, *The Fool of the World and the Flying Ship.* CM
> A story retold by Arthur Rackham.

Alvin Tresselt, *White Snow, Bright Snow.* CM
> Puts into words and pictures the marvel of a snowfall.

_____, *Hide and Seek Fog,* il. Roger Duvoisin.

_____, *The Mitten,* il. Yaroslava.
> An old Ukranian folk tale.

Janice Udry, *A Tree Is Nice,* il. Marc Simont. CM
> Simple, but elegant—the delights of a tree.

_____, *What Mary Jo Shared.*

_____, *The Moon Jumpers,* il. Maurice Sendak.

_____, *Let's Be Enemies,* il. Maurice Sendak.

Brian Wildsmith, *Birds.*
> A stare of owls. A fall of woodcocks. Learning about birds.

_____, *The Bremen Town Band.*
> Donkey, dog, rooster, and cat set off to become musicians.

_____, *The Apple Bird.*

_____, *Amazing World of Words.*

_____, *Carousel.*

_____, *Can You Do This?*

_____, *Reading.*

_____, *Exodus.*

_____, *Joseph.*
> Dozens of his brightly illustrated books are constantly being reissued.

Charlotte Zolotow, *The Sleepy Book,* il. Stefano Vitale.

> Just right for reading at bedtime.

_____, *William's Doll*, il. William Pene DuBois.

> William wants a doll so he can practice being a father.

_____, *I Like to Be Little*, il. Erik Bleqvad.

> A little girl explains why to her mother.

_____, *When the Wind Stops*, il. Stefano Vitale.

> Where does the sun go when the day ends? Where does the wind go?

_____, *Do You Know What I'll Do?* il. Javaka Steptoe.

> A 1958 classic with new illustrations featuring African-American characters.

_____, *The Seashore Book.*

_____, *The Storm Book.*

_____, *Over and Over.*

_____, *The Quarreling Book.*

_____, *Mr. Rabbit and the Lovely Present.*

_____, *The Quiet Lady.*

> Charlotte Zolotow is a legend in children's books.

From *Rain Rain Rivers*, written and illustrated by Uri Shulevitz. Copyright © 1969. Reproduced by permission of Farrar, Straus & Giroux, Inc.

Frogs,
stop your croaking!
Take cover in the water
and listen to the rain.

"Just stop the pain," whimpered the fox, wiping some tears away. Despite his misery, he realized he had a tasty little morsel in his mouth, and his jaw began to quiver. "Keep open!" yelled Doctor De Soto. "Wide open!" yelled his wife.

Chapter 13

More Favorite Picture Books: Ages 4–8

Of the making of wonderful picture books there is no end! Some of these, in print for over twenty-five years, are on the way to becoming classics. Their author/illustrators qualify as national treasures, like William Steig, Barbara Cooney, Tomie dePaola, David Small, Brinton Turkle, Chris Van Allsburg, Tasha Tudor, Peter Spier, Bernard Waber, and numerous others.

Since a list of more than a hundred author/illustrators is hard to handle, I tried to think of a way to divide this list into categories. I chose subject headings, listing books under each heading alphabetically by author. This may be confusing because the category is based on the first book mentioned. Almost all author/illustrators have several books mentioned, and nearly all of their books are on different subjects than the category indicates. What to do?

First of all, don't get stuck on the category. Look for books in all of them, and particularly look for author/illustrators that you like. Don't let the first book listed keep you from investigating the others! The number of picture books published each year is overwhelming; this list represents the best we found.

Discovering the World and Myself

Edward Ardizzone, *Little Tim and the Brave Sea Captain.*
> The words and pictures combine to tell an exciting story of going to sea.

Mary Brigid Barrett, *Sing to the Stars*, il. Sandra Speidel.
> A young violinist is surprised twice in this story when he learns that music is best experienced when shared with others.

Marie Bradley, *More Than Anything in the World,* il. Chris K. Soentpiet.
> Told in his own voice, nine-year-old Booker T. Washington longs to learn to read.

Rebecca Caudill, *A Pocketful of Cricket.* CH
> A pet cricket goes to school in a boy's pocket.

_____, *The Best-Loved Doll.*
> The prize is given for the oldest, best-dressed doll, but Betsy wins with her patched-up best-loved doll.

Bryan Collier, *Uptown.* CSK
> What a view of Harlem! It dazzles from cover to cover.

Barbara Cooney, *Chanticleer and the Fox.* CM
> Geoffrey Chaucer's "Nun's Priest Tale" adapted by the illustrator.

_____, *Island Boy.* BG/HB
> The lovely story of a boy's life and his attachment to the island.

_____, *Miss Rumphius.*
> Miss Rumphius leaves a legacy of beauty by sowing bushels of lupines in her travels.

Niki Daly, *Not So Fast, Songolo.*
> "Not so fast, Songolo," Grandmother says as they travel home after buying Malusi a pair of much-admired red sneakers.

_____, *Jamela's Dress.*
> Jamela gets carried away with the beauty of her mother's dress fabric as it dries on the line and wears it herself.

_____, *Papa Lucky's Shadow.*
> All of these stories have a South African setting.

Tomie dePaola, *The Art Lesson.*

> Autobiographical account of a boy name Tommy who wants to be an artist.

_____, *Now One Foot, Now the Other.*

_____, *Nana Upstairs and Nana Downstairs.*

> Two delightful stories about helping aging family members.

Mem Fox, *Wilfrid Gordon McDonald Partridge,* il. Julie Vivas.

> Heartwarming story of a small boy who lives next to an "old people's home." What is a memory, anyhow? Vivas is an award-winning artist not to be missed.

_____, *Time for Bed.*

_____, *Wombat Divine,* il. Kerry Argent.

Wilfrid Gordon McDonald Partridge, by Mem Fox, il. Julie Vivas.
Copyright © 1985. Used by permission of Kane/Miller.

Patricia Lee Gauch, ***Christina Katerina and the Box,***
il. Doris Burn.
A young girl with good imagination turns a big box into many
things.
_____, *Christina Katerina and Fats and the Great Neighborhood War.*
Christina Katerina has many adventures in other books.
_____, *Presenting Tanya the Ugly Duckling,* il. Satomi Ichikawa.
An emerging ballerina, Tanya believes she is like the ugly
duckling. How will she ever get the dance steps right?
Delicate pastel drawings by Ichikawa.
_____, *Noah,* il. Jonathan Green.
Noah is portrayed as an ebony-skinned herdsman of the African
savannah. The biblical story is told in lyrical, rhythmic prose.

Donna Green, ***My Little Artist.***
Artistic heritage passed from grandmother to granddaughter.
Green's use of light is captivating.

Amy Hest, ***When Jessie Came Across the Sea,*** il. P. J. Lynch.
A beautifully illustrated book about Jessie's life as an immigrant
and her adjustment to New York City at the peak of European
immigration. We take so many things for granted.
_____, *The Friday Nights of Nana,* il. Claire A. Nivola.
The celebration of the Sabbath in a Jewish home.

Deborah Hopkinson, ***A Band of Angels,*** il. Raúl Colón.
Inspired by the Jubilee Singers of Fisk University, this book
sings out hope and freedom.
_____, *Sweet Clara and the Freedom Quilt.*
_____, *Birdie's Lighthouse.*

Gloria Houston, ***My Great Aunt Arizona,*** il. Susan Condie Lamb.
A bright pioneer girl's struggle to become a teacher. Her goal:
every pupil to see all the faraway places in the world someday.
_____, *The Year of the Perfect Christmas Tree,* il. Barbara Cooney.
Set in Appalachia, with drawings from award-winning artist
Barbara Cooney, a story of tradition, struggle, song, and
surprise.

Jan Karon, ***Miss Fannie's Hat,*** il. Toni Goffe.
A story based on the author's wonderful hat-loving
grandmother.

Kevin Lewis, *The Lot at the End of My Block,* il. Reg Cartwright.

A delightful story of a small city boy watching a construction crew build an apartment dwelling where another boy will live and become his friend.

_____, *Chugga-Chugga Choo-Choo.*

Paul Owen Lewis, *Davy's Dream: A Young Boy's Adventure with Wild Orca Whales.*

Not to be missed! Lewis is a great "teller," and if you close your eyes, you may see "the wolves of the sea." Boys will want this one "again, please."

David McPhail, *Mole Music.*

Mole takes up the violin but never plays for an audience. Or does he?

_____, *Edward and the Pirates.*

While reading about lost pirate treasures, Edward finds himself surrounded by sailors who want him to read aloud to them in hopes of discovering the treasure.

_____, *The Puddle.*

_____, *Those Can-Do Pigs.*

McPhail's versatile porkers show up in several books.

_____, *Sisters.*

McPhail's imaginative drawings pull children into the story.

Lauren Mills, *The Rag Coat.*

Minna wants to go to school like other kids her age, but she is poor and has no coat. When the "Quilting Mothers" make her one, she finds that school is more than she expected.

Margaree King Mitchell, *Granddaddy's Gift,* il. Larry Johnson.

The characteristics of courage, determination, and studiousness are displayed in this story of freedom for a young African-American grandchild.

_____, *Uncle Jed's Barbershop*, il. James Ransome.

A lifelong dream achieved at the age of seventy-nine! Brightly stroked by artist Ransome.

Lloyd Moss, *Zin! Zin! Zin! A Violin,* il. Marjorie Priceman.

Whimsical drawings, counting, and rhyme introduce ten musical instruments and finally the whole orchestra.

Evaline Ness, *Sam, Bangs, and Moonshine.* CM
> Samantha learns that fantasy can have real consequences when she unwittingly jeopardizes the life of her friend Thomas and her cat Bangs.

_____, *Tom Tit Tot: An English Folk Tale.* CH
> A small, magical creature offers to help with a young woman's impossible sewing project, much like his distant cousin Rumplestiltskin.

Jenni Overend, *Welcome with Love,* il. Julie Vivas.
> Child number four is about to be born. The whole family is ready as is the midwife and Auntie Meg. Vivas' work is full of wonder and awe. Please be advised that the whole birth process is painted in these pages.

Brian Pinkney, *Max Found Two Sticks.*
> A delightful look at how music begins. Max finds scrub buckets, hat boxes, and empty soda bottles to tap on with his two sticks, and finally creates a marching band.

Patricia Polacco, *Chicken Sunday.*
> Two girls raise money to buy Miss Eula an Easter bonnet to thank her for the wonderful Sunday chicken dinners.

_____, *Just Plain Fancy.*
> Naomi and Ruth, two Amish girls, find an unusual egg and place it under a hen, only to find a pretty fancy bird hatching from their efforts.

_____, *The Keeping Quilt.*
> "We will make a quilt to help us always remember home."

_____, *Pink and Say.*
> A powerful story about two fifteen-year-old Union soldiers in the Civil War, one black, one white.

_____, *Rechenka's Eggs.*
> A delightful story of an old Babushka and a wounded goose.

_____, *Thank You, Mr. Falker.*
> Polacco dedicated this book to her fifth-grade teacher, who helped her overcome reading difficulties. Many of Polacco's heart-warming stories reflect her Russian background and come from her own life.

_____, *Thundercakes.*
> A little girl overcomes her fear of thunder with the help of her grandmother.

Katherine Potter, *Spike.*

>   Jackson, a quiet, overlooked boy both at home and school, draws
>   a stick figure which comes alive and calls himself Spike, setting
>   Jackson's world topsy-turvy and freeing him to express himself.

Allen Say, *Grandfather's Journey.* CM

>   A poignant story of Say's grandfather who loved two countries,
>   Japan and the United States.

_____, *Tea with Milk.*

_____, *Tree of Cranes.*

April Pulley Sayre, *It's My City! A Singing Map,* il. Denis Roche.

>   All the sights and sounds of a city go into this helpful and
>   creative map.

Laura Segal, *All the Way Home,* il. James Marshall.

>   Little Juliet falls in the park, and on her way home all the creatures
>   form a sympathetic parade to comfort the howling child.

Pegi Deitz Shea, *The Whispering Cloth,* il. Anita Riggio, stitched
by You Yang.

>   Set in a refuge camp, a Hmong girl learns how to make the
>   pandau ("flowery cloth") from her grandmother. Her first cloth
>   may make enough to give them a future. What is it worth?

William Steig, *Pete's a Pizza.*

>   Steig's commentary on raising children. All of Steig's books
>   have a clever twist that makes you think and smile over the
>   ridiculous.

_____, *Sylvester and the Magic Pebble.* CM

>   A lion frightens Sylvester on his way home after he finds a magic
>   pebble, and he makes a wish that brings unexpected results.

_____, *Yellow and Pink.*

>   Two marionettes discuss their origin: pink believes someone
>   made them; yellow thinks they happened by accident. Pink
>   wins. A subtle discussion about our origins.

_____, *The Amazing Bone.*

_____, *Amos and Boris.*

_____, *Brave Irene.*

_____, *Dominic.*

_____, *Dr. DeSoto.* BG/HB

_____, *Zeke Pippin.*

BG/HB	Boston Globe/Horn Book award
CM	Caldecott Medal
CH	Caldecott Honor
CSK	Coretta Scott King award
NA	Newbery Award
NH	Newbery Honor
NM	Newbery Medal

She even read while
Exercising,
And standing on her head.

Illustration from THE LIBRARY by Sarah Stewart, pictures by David Small.
Pictures copyright © 1995 by David Small.

Sarah Stewart, ***The Gardener,*** il. David Small. CH
> A little girl changes life in the city with her gardening skills.

_____, *The Journey*, il. David Small.
> The diary of an Amish girl whose visit to Chicago reminds her of what is true everywhere.

_____, *The Library*, il. David Small.
> Elizabeth Brown is a book lover and fills her house to the ceiling with books.

Gilles Tibo, ***The Cowboy Kid,*** il. Tom Kapas.
> Every boy's dream come true, yet even more than a "ride 'em cowboy" story.

Brinton Turkle, ***Deep in the Forest.***
> A retelling of Goldilocks and the Three Bears.

_____, *Do Not Open*.
> Following a storm, Miss Moody and her cat find a bottle washed ashore with a warning, "Do Not Open."

_____, *Thy Friend Obadiah*.
> A little Quaker boy on Nantucket becomes a friend of a seagull he helps.

Ann Turner, ***Through Moon and Stars and Night Skies,*** il. James Graham Hale.
> Very tender story of an adopted child's trip across the sea to meet his new parents.

_____, *In the Heart*, il. Salley Mavor.
> In this striking book, the author asks what is the heart of a kitchen, a town, or an afternoon? Mavor has a style all her own, incorporating materials and fabric.

_____, *Drummer Boy*.

Chris Van Allsburg, ***The Polar Express.*** CM
> Late one Christmas Eve a boy boards a mysterious train bound for the North Pole.

_____, *Jumanji*. CM
> A brother and sister discover a magic board game that wreaks havoc in the house.

_____, *The Garden of Abdul Gasazi*. CH BG/HB
> While baby-sitting the neighbor's dog, a boy stumbles upon a magic garden.

_____, *The Stranger*.

_____, *The Wreck of the Zephyr*.

Jean Van Leeuwen, *Emma Bean,* il. Juan Wijngaard.
"Once there was a rabbit who had a girl . . ." Van Leeuwen is a versatile writer of over thirty children's books.

_____, *Across the Wide Sea.*

_____, *The Tickle Stories.*

_____, *Wait for Me Said Maggie McGee.*

Leatie Weiss, *My Teacher Sleeps in School,* il. Ellen Weiss.
The children are suspicious! Teacher is there when they arrive and stays after they leave.

David Wiesner, *Tuesday.* CM
At dusk on Tuesday frogs take to the air and enjoy the neighborhood till dawn. Wiesner is a brilliant artist whose imagination is thrilling.

_____, *Sector Seven.* CH
A field trip to the Empire State Building turns into a cloudy adventure.

_____, *Hurricane.*

_____, *June 29, 1999.*

_____, *The Three Pigs.*

Taro Yashima, *Crow Boy.* CH
Chibi, a shy boy, is shunned by his classmates until he is discovered by his teacher, who helps the class accept someone who is different.

_____, *The Umbrella.*
Momo waits eagerly for a rainy day so she can use her new red boots and umbrella.

Cuddly Books for Bedtime or Any Time

Cecil Frances Alexander, *All Things Bright and Beautiful,*
il. Bruce Whatley.

Jim Aylesworth, *The Bad Dream,* il. Judithe Friedman.
This one will come in handy for those bad-dream fears.

_____, *Jim Aylesworth's Book of Bedtime Stories,* various illustrators.
Four delightfully soothing stories that will bring comfort through the night.

Helen E. Buckley, *Grandfather and I,* il. Jan Ormerod.
_____, *Grandmother and I.*
> Two loving African-American families and close-up looks at
> a child's relationship with grandparents.

Miriam Cohen, *Will I Have a Friend?* il. Lillian Hoban.
> Jim is anxious about entering school and needs assurance.

_____, *So What?*
_____, *Welcome to First Grade.*
_____, *Best Friends.*

Jim didn't know.

"The answer is—a milk truck!" Paul said.

They all laughed. It was a good riddle.

From *The New Teacher* by Miriam Cohen, illustrated by Lillian Hoban. Copyright ©
1972 by Macmillan Publishing Co., Inc. Reprinted with permission of the publisher.

Marla Frazee, *Hush, Little Baby: A Folk Song.*
> Wonderfully illustrated story in the Appalachian time period of the lullaby's birth.

Elizabeth Hill, *Evan's Corner,* il. Sandra Speidel.
> Even in a small apartment a child needs a place of his own.

Nancy Jewell, *Sailor Song,* il. Stefano Vitale.
> A mother sings her son a lullaby about his father's return from the sea.

Robert Munsch, *Love You Forever,* il. Sheila McGraw.
> Read the world over, expressing a family's unending love.

_____, *Thomas's Snowsuit.*

Peter Spier, *Noah's Ark.*
> Peter Spier's books are alive with imagination. Ageless!

_____, *Christmas.*
_____, *People.*
_____, *The Book of Jonah.*
_____, *Circus.*
_____, *The Star-Spangled Banner.*

Eileen Spinelli, *Somebody Loves You, Mr. Hatch,* il. Paul Yalowitz.
> Reclusive Mr. Hatch receives an anonymous Valentine that changes his life and neighborhood. Note the artist's use of color, page after page.

_____, *Sophie's Masterpiece,* il. Jane Dyer.
> A spider that is always being shooed away looks for her niche. Who will let her create?

_____, *Night Shift Daddy.*

Tasha Tudor, *Corgiville Fair.*
> Sights and fun of a small-town fair and a goat race with Tudor's wonderful pictures.

_____, *1 is One.* CH
_____, *A is for Annabelle: A Doll's Alphabet.*
_____, *First Prayers.*

Bernard Waber, *Ira Sleeps Over.*
> Invited to sleep over at a friend's home, Ira wonders if he should take his teddy bear.

_____, *Lyle, Lyle Crocodile.*
>   A series about a pet crocodile.

Vera B. Williams, *A Chair for My Mother.*
>   A story of a child's sacrifice for a hard-working mother.

_____, *Stringbean's Trip to the Shining Sea.*
>   Stringbean and his brother send postcards back home on their trip to the Pacific Ocean, making this story a gentle geography lesson.

From *And So It Was,* illustrated by Tasha Tudor.
Copyright © MCMLVIII, by W. L. Jenkins.
Used by permission of The Westminster Press.

Stories About Animals

Jon Agee, *Milo's Hat Trick.*
> Milo is a magician in need of a new trick—quick. He snags a bear for his act.

John Burningham, *Mr. Gumpy's Outing.*
> A series of books about Mr. Gumpy, the children, and farm animals.

_____, *John Patrick Norman McHennessy—The Boy Who Was Always Late.*

Jean de Brunhoff, *Bonjour, Babar!*
> Six stories in a new gift edition, full of adventure and fantasy, bring back these wonderful elephant stories from a French author who died in 1937.

Russell Hoban, *Bedtime for Frances,* il. Garth Williams.

_____, *Bread and Jam for Frances,* il. Lillian Hoban.

_____, *A Baby Sister for Frances*, il. Lillian Hoban.
> A series about lovable badger Frances, full of tricks and good lessons. These classics from a British author will be part of your child's life forever.

Holly Hobbie, *Toot and Puddle.*
> Meet a friendship of opposites at work. Share in the adventures of homebody Puddle and world traveler Toot. Hobbie's series is pensive, yet humorous.

_____, *A Present for Toot.*

_____, *You Are My Sunshine.*

Leo Lionni, *Frederick.*
> Foolish Frederick doesn't gather for winter like other mice, but reads poetry to the other mice during a long winter. Frederick has many other adventures.

_____, *Swimmy.* CH
> The heroic deeds of a little black fish with beautiful seascape drawings.

_____, *Alexander and the Wind-Up Mouse.*
> The story of a friendship between a real mouse and a wind-up mouse.

_____, *Inch by Inch*.
> Winsome inchworm proves his ability to measure anything under the sun.

_____, *Fish Is Fish*.
> A minnow wants to follow a tadpole out of the pond to become a frog.

Janet Marshall, *A Honey of a Day*.
> Intriguing use of twenty-eight flower names for animals who take part in a wedding day.

James Marshall, *George and Martha*, il. Maurice Sendak.
> These two friendly hippos are back in print. Your kids will love them.

Patricia C. McKissack, *Flossie and the Fox*, il. Rachel Isadora.
> Small Flossie outwits a wily fox determined to steal her eggs.

_____, *Ma Dear's Aprons*, il. Floyd Cooper.
> David Earl can tell the days of the week by the aprons Ma Dear wears.

_____, *The Honest-to-Goodness Truth*, il. Giselle Potter.
> Libby Louise learns the difference between the right and wrong way to tell the truth—the hard way.

Peggy Rathmann, *Officer Buckle and Gloria*. CM
> What better way to learn safety tip #101: Always stay with your buddy? Officer Buckle and dog Gloria will teach you how.

_____, *10 Minutes Till Bedtime*.
> As Dad counts down till bedtime, the hamster parade begins. Don't miss the tour.

Cynthia Rylant, *The Great Gracie Chase: Stop That Dog!*
il. Mark Teague.
> Gracie, a good and contented dog, starts barking when the painters come and she is put outside. That begins the adventure.

_____, *When I Was Young in the Mountains*, il. Diane Goode.
> Nostalgic journey through another time and place of strong family ties.

Illustration by Marc Simont from
The Stray Dog. Copyright © 2001.
Used by permission of HarperCollins.

_____, *In November*, il. Judith Kastner.
"In November the smell of food is different. It is an orange smell. A squash and pumpkin smell." A mood book with superb illustrations.

_____, *Thimbleberry Stories*, il. Maggie Kneen.
Four short stories about the life of Nigel Chipmunk.

Marc Simont, *The Stray Dog.*
A stray dog, a picnic in the country, a return to find the stray dog they have already named Willy. Your kids will love it!

Lynd Ward, *The Biggest Bear.* CM
Johnny wanted a bearskin on his barn, so he goes looking for the biggest bear.

_____, *The Silver Pony.*
A classic wordless book about a lonely farm boy.

Stories that Make Us Laugh

Ted Arnold, *Parts.*
Comical! What's a five-year-old to think when his hair, skin, and teeth come out?

_____, *The Signmaker's Assistant.*
Little Norman turns the town upside down while his boss is away.

_____, *No Jumping on the Bed.*

Judi Barrett, *Cloudy with a Chance of Meatballs,* il. Ron Barrett.
How bizarre to have your meals pouring down from the sky three times a day.

_____, *Pickles to Pittsburgh*, a sequel.

Ludwig Bemelmans, *Madeline.* CM
Inimitable Madeline's adventures are largely French and the series is hilarious reading. This story has delighted generations of readers.

Roger Duvoisin, *Petunia*.

The story of a silly goose who thought possession of a book made her wise.

Ian Falconer, *Olivia*.

Olivia rocks! She's one hilarious six-year-old pig. Look out, Broadway.

_____, *Olivia Saves the Circus*.

Olivia is Queen of the Trampoline until her porcine self is caught in the safety net.

Jules Feiffer, *Bark, George*.

Hilarious story about a dog whose bark, well, isn't one. What a discovery at the vet's!

_____, *I Lost My Bear*.

The search for a lost bear is overwhelmed by everything else that is found!

_____, *Meanwhile*.

Kevin Henkes, *Owen*. CH

Young mouse is about to attend school but won't go without his blanket. Mom's creative solution saves the day.

_____, *SHHHH*.

What happens when a toddler wakes up before everyone else in the family?

_____, *Lilly's Purple Plastic Purse*.

Hilarious antics of Lilly and her classy new purse.

_____, *Sheila Rae, the Brave*.

_____, *Chrysanthemum*.

_____, *Chester's Way*.

Hilary Knight, *Where's Wallace?*

An orangutan escapes from the zoo; maybe you can find him.

Helen Lester, *Tacky the Penguin*, il. Lynn Munsinger.

Tacky is an exuberant penguin living with peers Goodly, Lovely, Angel, Neatly, and Perfect, who consider him an "odd bird, but a nice bird to have around."

_____, *Three Cheers for Tacky*.

_____, *Tacky in Trouble*.

_____, *Tacky and the Emperor*.

David Macaulay, *Why the Chicken Crossed the Road.*
> This book answers the question, "Do you have a really funny book?"

Susan Meddaugh, *Martha Speaks.*
> Martha, the dog, learns to talk by swallowing alphabet soup.

_____, *Martha Walks the Dog.*
> Martha tries to rehabilitate antisocial canines. Actually, Martha has a series of stories about her giftedness.

Bill Peet, *Bufford, the Little Bighorn.*

_____, *Caboose Who Got Loose.*

_____, *Kermit the Hermit.*
> Whatever you find by Bill Peet will set your children laughing.

Lisa Westburg Peters, *Cold Little Duck, Duck, Duck,* il. Sam Williams.
> When a duck returns to a frozen pond too early in the season, a friendly bear tells her to go "back, back, back." But duck "thinks, thinks, thinks" of spring. Invites letter–word recognition.

Marjorie Priceman, *Emeline at the Circus.*
> Emeline's antics prove to be the best of the show, much to her teacher's horror.

John A. Rowe, *Baby Crow.*
> A baby crow wants to be a great opera singer but can't say "caw."

Dr. Seuss, *The Cat in the Hat.*

_____, *Horton Hatches an Egg.*

_____, *Green Eggs and Ham.*
> The list of Dr. Seuss's wacky books could go on and on—all are fun ways to try out language and rhymes.

David Shannon, *No, David.*
> Shannon has taken the "no" word seriously with his unique brand of art.

_____, *David Goes to School.*

_____, *A Bad Case of Stripes.*

James Stevenson, *Don't Make Me Laugh.*
> Mr. Frimdimpy, a gloomy, bossy alligator, lays down the rules for this book: "Don't Laugh!" "Don't Smile!"

Tomi Ungerer, *Crictor*.

> A hilarious story of a boa constrictor who is the pet of an elderly French school mistress.

_____, *The Beast of Monsieur Racine*.

_____, *No Kiss for Mother*.

Nancy Willard, *The High Rise Glorious Skittle Skat Roarious Sky Pie Angel Food Cake*.

_____, *The Nightgown of the Sullen Moon*.

Gene Zion, *Harry the Dirty Dog* and other adventures,
il. Margaret Bloy Graham.

> This dog and laughter go together.

Noticing the World Around Us

Molly Bang, *Goose*.

> A baby goose adopted by woodchucks at birth has the feeling she doesn't belong.

Janell Cannon, *Stellaluna*.

> Delightful, educational, and witty story of a fruit bat. Well-crafted prose and stunning art.

_____, *Verdi*.

> Likely to make anyone a snake lover! Verdi struggles to prevent his inevitable lifestyle.

_____, *Trupp*.

_____, *Crickwing*.

Estelle Condra, *See the Ocean*, il. Linda Crockett-Blassingame.

> On the yearly trip over the mountains to the sea, Nellie's brothers compete to be first to see the ocean. One year, from the middle of the backseat, Nellie joins in with a striking view of the sea.

Pam Conrad, *The Rooster's Gift*, il. Eric Beddows.

> Does the Rooster really bring the morning? Small Hen and Rooster discover what gifts really are. Beddows' art is like the dawn itself.

Lisa Campbell Ernst, *Bubba and Trixie.*
> Come see the garden in a whole new way as this caterpillar and ladybug grow up and take you on the ride of your imaginative life.

_____, *Stella LouElla's Runaway Book.*

Marie H. Ets, *Gilberto and the Wind.*
> A little boy learns where the wind goes and what it does.

_____, *Play with Me.*

_____, *Just Me.*

May Garelick, *Where Does the Butterfly Go When It Rains?*
> il. Nicholas Wilton.
> Every animal has a place to hide when it rains, but what about butterflies?

_____, *What Makes a Bird a Bird?*

_____, *Look at the Moon.*

Donald Hall, *The Ox-Cart Man,* il. Barbara Cooney. CM
> A gentle story of a farmer's trip to market.

_____, *The Farm Summer 1942,* il. Barry Moser.
> A delicious look at rural life in a seemingly simpler world.

Karen Hesse, *Come On, Rain!* il. John J. Muth.
> After weeks without a summer rain, celebrate the joys of dancing in the rain in your bathing suit on a hot summer day.

Mick Inkpen, *Penguin Small.*
> Meet a penguin afraid of the water and find out how he makes it to the South Pole. Enjoy Inkpen's fanciful art.

_____, *Kipper's Toybox.*

_____, *Kipper's Snowy Day.*

_____, *Kipper's Birthday.*

D. B. Johnson, *Henry Hikes to Fitchburg.* BG/HB
> Come take a thirty-mile walk; or would you rather take the train? A playful introduction to the life of Thoreau.

Natalie Kinsey-Warnock, *The Bear That Heard Crying,*
> il. Ted Rand.
> In the woods of New Hampshire, a three-year-old girl is lost. Based on true events in 1783, Kinsey-Warnock makes vivid the long four-day search.

_____, *Fiddler of the Northern Lights,* il. Leslie W. Bowman.
> Grandpa's story about the Northern Lights with Bowman's star-skating illustrations.

_____, *On a Starry Night,* il. David McPhail.

_____, *A Farm of Her Own,* il. Kathleen Kolb.

David Kirk, *Miss Spider's Tea Party.*
> Counting, poetry, bugs, colors, and lots of emoting—it's all here. Kirk has created a character whose desire is to make friends. Kirk has a series about Miss Spider.

Jacqueline Briggs Martin, *Snowflake Bentley,* il. Mary Azarian. CM
> Bentley discovered, through study and photography, that each snowflake is a unique creation.

Barbara Mitchell, *Waterman's Child,* il. Daniel San Souci.
> Looking through the eyes of children, Mitchell pens the sights and smells of the fishing industry of Tilghaman Island in Chesapeake Bay.

L. Joanne Ryder, *The Waterfall's Gift,* il. Richard Jesse Watson.
> Grandpa always said, "The old north woods hides treasure in its deepest places." With absorbing illustrations and childhood awe of nature, the author masterfully weaves grief and renewal together for one young girl.

_____, *My Father's Hands.*

_____, *Dancers in the Garden.*

Scott Russell Sanders, *Meeting Trees,* il. Robert Hynes.
> Come play a game in the woods with a carpenter and his son. Hynes's art tingles the senses.

_____, *Aurora Means Dawn.*

Jan Thornhill, *Before and After.*
> Marvelous pictures and timescapes of nature changing by the moment, day, or season. A *National Geographic* book.

Martin Waddell, *The Big, Big Sea,* il. Jennifer Eachus.
> The sea is magical in the moonlight as a little girl and her mother splash in the moon path in the water.

_____, *Good Job, Little Bear.*

_____, *You and Me, Little Bear.*

Jane Yolen, *Owl Moon*, il. John Schoenherr. CM
> Shadows in the woods are very black. When you go owling you have to be brave, even when you are with your father.

_____, *Letting Swift River Go.*
_____, *All Those Secrets of the World.*
_____, *Off We Go.*

Legends and Tales from Other Times and Places

Verna Aardema, *Why Mosquitoes Buzz in People's Ears*, il. Leo and Diane Dillon. CM
> A retelling of an African tale with unusual illustrations.

_____, *The Lonely Lioness and the Ostrich Chicks.*
> A Masai fable.

Jan Brett, *The Mitten*.
> Brett's use of borders to peek ahead is intriguing. She retells an old Ukrainian Tale.

_____, *Annie and the Wild Animals.*
_____, *Berlioz the Bear.*
_____, *The Hat.*
_____, *Gingerbread Baby.*
_____, *The Twelve Days of Christmas.*
_____, *The Night Before Christmas.*

Marcia Brown, *Dick Whittington and His Cat*. CH
> The well-loved tale of the London waif whose cat's prowess as a ratter results in his becoming the Lord Mayor of London.

_____, *Stone Soup.* CH
> An old tale about the lessons three soldiers taught the villagers.

_____, *Once a Mouse.* CM
> A story of a lion who refused to believe he was once a mouse.

Jeff Brumbeau, *The Quiltmaker's Gift*, il. Gail de Marcken.
> A splendid tale of a greedy king too rich to receive a quilt from the quiltmaker. How will he get what he wants?

Thornton W. Burgess, *Old Mother West Wind*, il. Michael Hague.
_____, *Mother West Wind's Children.*

_____, *Mother West Wind's Neighbors.*

> Published in 1910, newly illustrated. This delightful storybook has timeless tales in chapter form to delight 4–8 year olds. Good to read aloud.

Brock Cole, *The King at the Door.*
_____, *Buttons.* BG/HB

> Two delectable tales that teach a lesson, illustrated with Cole's lively pen drawings. All ages.

Phoebe Gilman, *Something from Nothing.*

> A traditional Jewish tale of a boy's blanket creatively changed by Grandpa's tailoring skills until finally Joseph has his own idea of transformation.

Margaret Hodges, *Saint George and the Dragon,*
> il. Trina Schart Hyman. CM

Ellen Howard, *The Log Cabin Quilt,* il. Ronald Himler.

> A frontier story with clever children who use scraps of material to chink the new log cabin and keep warm.

Charles Kingsley, *The Water-Babies,* il. Charles Kingsley;
> new edition, il. Jessie Willcox Smith.
> Since it was first published in 1863 this story of Tom, a chimney sweep, has been a juvenile classic.

Julius Lester, reteller, *Uncle Remus: The Complete Tales,*
> il. Jerry Pinkney.
> Stories of Brer Rabbit friends, these were originally written over a hundred years ago by Joel Chandler Harris.
_____, *John Henry.*
_____, *Black Cowboy, Wild Horses.*

Will Moses, *Rip Van Winkle.*

> A retelling of Washington Irving's story illustrated with primitive paintings in the style of Grandma Moses by one of her offspring.

John Steptoe, *Mufaro's Beautiful Daughters: An African Tale.* BG/HB
> A Cinderella-like tale about two sisters and a young king searching for a bride.

Picture Books for Adults Who Haven't Completely Grown Up

Eileen Christelow, *The Five-Dog Night.*

Lisa Campbell Ernst, *Goldilocks Returns.*

Leo and Diane Dillon, *To Every Thing There Is a Season.*

Donald Hall, *I Am the Dog/I Am the Cat,* il. Barry Moser.

Barry Moser, *The Three Little Pigs.*

Jill Murphy, *Five Minutes' Peace.*

Dr. Seuss, *Oh, The Places You'll Go!*

Jeanne and William Steig, *A Handful of Beans: Six Fairy Tales.*

William Steig, *Made for Each Other.*

Judith St. George, *So You Want to be President?* il. David Small. CM

Earnest Thayer, *Casey at the Bat,* il. Christopher Bing. CH

Priscilla Turner, *The War Between the Vowels and the Consonants,* il. Whitney Turner.

Chris Van Allsburg, *The Mysteries of Harris Burdick.*

Judith Viorst, *Alexander and the Terrible, Horrible, No Good, Very Bad Day,* il. Ray Cruz.

Chapter 14

First Books for Beginning Readers

I feel a "goose-bumpy" kind of pleasure when I watch children learning to read. It never seems ordinary or "expected" to me, even though millions learn to read each year. For me it is seeing the miracle repeated: small human beings equipped by God take letter sounds and make them into words, begin to recognize letter combinations, and suddenly enter the world of words and imagination and ideas. These shining symbols known as words are uniquely owned by human beings.

When reading readiness begins—at whatever age—it is important for parents to sit and listen, to participate in the adventure. It may be time-consuming because the young reader is confronting new words on every page. Helping a beginning reader takes time; you have to be purposeful and patient. Learning to read is an exercise that sets a child off on the right course in relating to the world and all the wonders in it. I think of Ruth Love, onetime superintendent of Chicago schools, who said that if parents would read with their children for fifteen minutes a day they could change the shape of the Chicago school system. I prefer to say that they could change the shape of a life!

If you have been reading picture books with your preschool children, you will find them picking up words from the repeated reading of their favorites. It takes some children longer than others to see how it works, but they will soon be reading those books themselves. The list that follows gives titles of books (and there are so many now!) that can inspire children to begin on their own. Some are chapter books—marvelous milestones for a child.

Level one indicates a simple vocabulary, with repeated words or phrases to help the reader. Level two indicates either a more advanced vocabulary or a beginner's chapter book.

David Adler, *Young Cam Jansen*, il. Susanne Natti. LEVEL 2
> Cam Jansen solves mysteries in this series of books.

Avi, *Finding Providence*, il. James Watling. LEVEL 2
> The true story of Roger Williams and the settlement in Providence told with verve.
_____, *Abigail Takes the Wheel*, il. Don Bolognese.
> Abigail takes the helm when the captain of the ship can no longer do so.

Norman Bridwell, *Clifford the Big Red Dog*. LEVEL 1
_____, *Clifford Makes a Friend*.
> Children read about the dog they may have met in board books.

Pat Brisson, *Hot Fudge Hero*, il. Diana Cain Bluthenthal. LEVEL 1
_____, *Little Sister, Big Sister*.
_____, *Bertie's Picture Day*.

Betsy Byars, *The Golly Sisters*, il. Susan G. Truesdell. LEVEL 2
> A series about the Golly sisters for young readers with Byars' hilarious characters and happenings.
_____, *My Brother Ant*, il. Marc Simont.
_____, *Ant Plays Bear*.
_____, *Little Horse*, il. David McPhail.

Eleanor Coerr, *Chang's Paper Pony*, il. Deborah Kogan Ray. LEVEL 2
> Chang and Grandpa work in the California Gold Rush (1850s), but Chang longs for a pony and finds a way to get one.
_____, *Buffalo Bill and the Pony Express*, il. Don Bolognese.

Tomie dePaola, *Mother Goose Favorites: The Easy-to-Read Little Engine That Could*, il. Watty Piper. LEVEL 1

P. D. Eastman, *Are You My Mother?* LEVEL 1
> A confused bird tries to find his identity.

_____, *Big Dog, Little Dog.*

_____, *Go, Dog, Go!*

_____, *The Best Nest.*

_____, *Flap Your Wings.*
> Eastman's books feature simple story lines with enough fun and repeated words to keep a child going.

Rita Golden Gilman, *More Spaghetti, I Say!* LEVEL 2
> Humorous rhymes.

Karen Hesse, *Sable,* il. Marcia Sewall. LEVEL 2
> Tate tries to keep her dog Sable from wandering. A wonderful dog story.

Amy Hest, *Pajama Party.* LEVEL 2
> Three girls plan their own sleepover.

Syd Hoff, *Danny and the Dinosaur.* LEVEL 1

_____, *Sammy the Seal.*
> Charmers. Capturing a word like *dinosaur* is quite an achievement.

Nancy Smiler Levinson, *Snowshoe Thompson,* il. Joan Sandin. LEVEL 2
> Postman Thompson designs a pair of skis so he can get over the Sierra Nevada Mountains to deliver mail to Danny's family.

Jean Little, *Emma's Magic Winter,* il. Jennifer Plecas. LEVEL 2
> Emma is too shy to speak above a whisper whenever it is her turn to read aloud in class until a new girl moves in next door and the magic of friendship begins.

_____, *Emma's Yucky Brother,* a sequel.

Star Livingstone, *Harley,* il. Molly Bang. LEVEL 2
> Harley, the llama, is a failure as a pack animal, but finds his true role shepherding sheep.

Arnold Lobel, *Frog and Toad Are Friends.* LEVEL 2 CH

_____, *Days with Frog and Toad.*

_____, *Frog and Toad All Year.*

_____, *Frog and Toad Together.* NH

_____, *Owl at Home.*

BG/HB	Boston Globe/Horn Book award
CM	Caldecott Medal
CH	Caldecott Honor
CSK	Coretta Scott King award
NA	Newbery Award
NH	Newbery Honor
NM	Newbery Medal

Mercer Mayer, *Little Critter's Read-It-Yourself Story Book.* LEVEL 2
Six easy-to-read stories.

David McPhail, *The Day No Sheep Showed Up.* LEVEL 2
The farm animals don't know what a sheep is!
_____, *A Bug, A Bear, and a Boy.* LEVEL 1

Else H. Minarik, *Little Bear,* il. Maurice Sendak. LEVEL 1
_____, *A Kiss for Little Bear.*
_____, *Father Bear Comes Home.*
_____, *Little Bear's Visit.*
_____, *Little Bear's Friend.*

Mary Pope Osborne, The Magic Tree House series. LEVEL 2
Jack and Annie have many magical adventures in this series
that has turned reluctant learners into readers.

Peggy Parish, *Thank You, Amelia Bedelia,* il. Fritz Siebel. LEVEL 2
Literal-minded Amelia prepares for a fussy aunt's visit by airing
the vegetables and separating the eggs. Beginning readers love
the wordplay.
_____, *Come Back, Amelia Bedelia,* il. Walter Tripp.
_____, *Amelia Bedelia and the Surprise Shower.*
A series that has kept children in giggles for years.

Cynthia Rylant, *Mr. Putter and Tabby,* il. Arthur Howard. LEVEL 1
_____, *Mr. Putter and Tabby Row the Boat.*
_____, *Mr. Putter and Tabby Toot the Horn.*
_____, *Mr. Putter and Tabby Take the Train.*
_____, *Mr. Putter and Tabby Walk the Dog.*
A series of humorous, delightful books children love with Mr.
Putter and his aging tabby cat.
_____, *The High-Rise Private Eyes,* il. G. Brian Karas. LEVEL 2
Bunny Brown is the brains of the duo; Jack Jones is the snoop,
and together they crack cases wide open in this series. The
illustrations help the reader look for clues.

Louis Sachar, *The Marvin Redpost Quartet,* il. Neal Hughes. LEVEL 2
Funny, easy-to-read books about a boy who is convinced he is
someone else.

Joan Sandin, *The Long Way to a New Land.* LEVEL 2
_____, *The Long Way Westward.*
Two books about a Swedish family's journey to a new home in
Minnesota.

Richard Scarry, ***Best Read-It-Yourself Book Ever.*** LEVEL 1
>   Twelve stories for new readers.

George Shea, ***First Flight: The Story of Tom Tate and the Wright Brothers,*** il. Don Bolognese. LEVEL 2

Jerry Spinelli, ***Tooter Pepperday,*** il. Donna Nelson. LEVEL 2
>   Tooter doesn't want to move to the farm, but along the way she begins to see life differently.

James Stevenson, ***Mud Flat April Fool.*** LEVEL 1
>   Easy vocabulary, short chapters; sure to tickle the funny bone.

Ann Warren Turner, ***Dust for Dinner,*** il. Robert Barrett. LEVEL 2
>   An Oklahoma family is displaced during the drought and dust storms.

Jenny Tyler, ***Ted in a Red Bed.*** LEVEL 1
>   A bear shops for a bed, falls asleep, and wonders how his bed got home.
_____, *Big Pig on a Dig.*

Jean Van Leeuwen, ***Two Girls in Sister Dresses,*** il. Linda Benson. LEVEL 2
_____, *Tales of Amanda Pig,* il. Ann Schweninger.
_____, *Tales of Oliver Pig.*

Gloria Whelan, ***Next Spring an Oriole.*** LEVEL 2
_____, *Night of the Full Moon.*
_____, *Shadow of the Wolf.*
>   Three stories of the pioneer adventures of ten-year-old Libby Mitchell and her family, who move by wagon from Virginia to settle on the Michigan frontier in the 1840s. Libby is mistakenly kidnapped, and her friendship with Fawn, a young Potawatomi Indian girl, changes her. Great chapter books.
_____, *Hannah.*
>   In 1887, the new teacher changes blind Hannah's life.
_____, Welcome to Starvation Lake series.
_____, *Silver.*
>   The story of an Alaskan girl's husky puppy.

Harriet Ziefert, ***The Cow in the House,*** il. Emily Bolan. LEVEL 1
>   What laughable confusion in one house!

From *Granfa' Grig Had a Pig* by Wallace Tripp.
Illustrations copyright © 1976 by Wallace Tripp.
Reproduced by permission of Little, Brown and Co.

Chapter 15

Classic Children's Novels: Ages 9–12

A classic is a book whose quality gives it an enduring lifespan. The book list for intermediate readers begins with titles that have been in print for at least fifty years. They demand a place of honor in a book list because they form a kind of reservoir of good reading for our culture. These books have influenced us more than we know; they remain relevant and timeless. And they are too good to let children overlook them in the rush for what is new.

BG/HB	Boston Globe/Horn Book award
CM	Caldecott Medal
CH	Caldecott Honor
CSK	Coretta Scott King award
NA	Newbery Award
NH	Newbery Honor
NM	Newbery Medal

Louisa May Alcott, *Little Women*.
> The well-loved story of family love, tragedy, and romance in the lives of the four March sisters. Wait until your child is twelve to read this.

_____, *Little Men*.
_____, *Jo's Boys*.

Richard and Florence Atwater, *Mr. Popper's Penguins*.
> House painter Mr. Popper's pet penguin becomes so lonely that Mr. Popper borrows a penguin from the zoo. It's enough to make you laugh!

Carol Ryrie Brink, *Caddie Woodlawn*, il. Trina Schart Hyman. NM
> Caddie, an impulsive, independent redheaded tomboy, finds adventure as she runs with her brothers in pioneer Wisconsin in the 1860s. Her mother, determined to turn her into a "lady," changes her mind when the settlers are faced with warring Indians. Caddie does what others are afraid to do—she goes off into the woods to talk with the Indians! Full of humor and fun, this book has impressed both boys and girls since 1936.

Frances Hodgson Burnett, *The Secret Garden*, il. Tasha Tudor.
> Mary Lennox changes the life of her cousin Colin and everyone in this joyless Victorian household with her creativity and work in the secret garden. A long-time favorite.

_____, *A Little Princess*.
> Young Sarah Crewe is sent from India by her father to live in a London boarding school, headed by the mean and imposing Miss Minchin. When her father's death leaves her destitute, she works as a servant to earn her keep. She is finally rescued by "magic" and united with a dear friend of her father's.

_____, *Little Lord Fauntleroy*.
> The tale of an American child who turns out to be an English nobleman. Sentimental and compellingly readable.

Alice Dalgleish, *The Bears on Hemlock Mountain*,
> il. Helen Sewell. NH
> Are there bears on Hemlock Mountain? A page-turner about a boy who found out.

_____, *The Courage of Sarah Noble.*
> Sarah goes to the wilds of Connecticut with her father and must remember her mother's words, "Keep your courage, Sarah!"

James Daugherty, *Daniel Boone.* NM
> A biography of every boy's hero, the king of the wild frontier.

Marguerite de Angeli, *The Door in the Wall.* NM
> A terrible illness leaves young Robin, a nobleman's son, crippled and abandoned, but Robin finds his destiny altered by his friendship with Brother Luke, a monk, who teaches him positive ways to endure what life may bring.

_____, *Thee Hannah!*
> An eight-year-old Quaker girl who longs for bright colors and lacy trim finds her plain gray bonnet gives courage for a runaway slave to ask for help.

Ingri and Edgar D'Aulaire, *Abraham Lincoln.* CM
> Beautifully written and illustrated life of Lincoln from his boyhood through his presidency. The D'Aulaires' biographies are worth looking for.

_____, *George Washington.*
_____, *Benjamin Franklin.*
_____, *Columbus.*

Meindert DeJong, *The Wheel on the School,* il. Maurice Sendak. NM
> Schoolchildren in a Dutch village use their ingenuity to bring the storks back to their island. Full of delight and insight.

William Pene DuBois, *The Twenty-One Balloons.* NM
> When Professor William Waterman Sherman was found adrift in the Atlantic clinging to the debris of his twenty-one balloons, all America was rocked with curiosity. Twelve and up.

Elizabeth Enright, *Then There Were Five.*
> The first in a series of four wonderful stories of the lively Melendy family, who invent the ISAAC—Independent Saturday Alternative Adventure Club. Favorites for well over fifty years.

_____, *The Saturdays.*
_____, *Spiderweb for Two.*
_____, *The Four-Story Mistake.*

_____, *Thimble Summer*. NM
> Ten-year-old Garnet Linden finds a thimble in the creek bottom and things begin to happen!

Eleanor Estes, *The Moffats,* a series, il. Louis Slobodkin. NH
> Four children and Mama—and their friends—have days packed full of fun and lively adventures despite a limited income. Long-time favorites.

_____, *Ginger Pye*. NM
> Ginger Pye, the smartest dog in the world, disappears on Thanksgiving Day, abducted by a stranger in a yellow hat, or so the children say.

_____, *The Hundred Dresses.*
> An immigrant child tells her class that she has one hundred fancy dresses at home, even though she wears the same faded blue dress every day.

Rachel Field, *Hitty, Her First Hundred Years.* NM
> A quaint story of a New England doll and her experiences. For readers beyond the doll age. A new edition by Rosemary Wells diminishes what makes Hitty unique. Look for the original and compare it yourself.

_____, *Calico Bush.*
> Maggie Ledoux, an indentured servant at age thirteen, travels to the New World from France with the Sargent family and proves her resilience and strength through the harsh winter of 1743 in northern Maine.

Dorothy Canfield Fisher, *Understood Betsy,* il. Eden Rose Lipson.
> A distinctive new edition of an old favorite written in 1916. Neurotic, sickly Elizabeth Ann grows healthy and happy when she is sent to a Vermont farm to live with no-nonsense relatives, the "dreaded Putneys," and learns to have fun.

Esther Forbes, *Johnny Tremain,* il. Michael McCurdy. NM
> A sumptuous new gift edition with vigorous woodcuts tells the story of a young silversmith's apprentice who chronicles the beginning of the Revolution in the American colonies.

_____, *America's Paul Revere*, il. Lynd Ward.
> Story about a well-known hero with background to the Revolutionary War.

Elizabeth Goudge, *Little White Horse*.

> Orphan Maria Merryweather (isn't that a great name?) arrives
> at Moonacre Manor with her governess to live with an elderly
> cousin. All sorts of unexplained things happen and, delving into
> them, Maria proceeds to change the life of almost everyone in
> this magical place. A lovely fairy tale—one of my favorites. All
> of Goudge's books cling to the heart.

_____, *The Blue Hills*.

> Everyone bound for the Blue Hills for a picnic celebrating
> Hugh Anthony's birthday gets lost on the way and experiences
> life-changing adventures. Recently reprinted.

Elizabeth Janet Gray, *Adam of the Road*. NM

> Adam, age eleven, has grown up traveling through the open
> roads of thirteenth-century England with his wandering
> minstrel father. When his father disappears, Adam is left alone.
> While searching for his father, Adam meets some endearing
> (and not so endearing) people and learns how others live.

Lucretia P. Hale, *The Complete Peterkin Papers*.

> For well over a hundred years children and parents have
> chuckled over the amusing incidents in the life of the zany
> Peterkin family, who manage to complicate even the simplest
> thing. First published in 1880!

Jesse Jackson, *Call Me Charley*.

> One of the first books to call all readers to attention about a
> boy and his black identity. A low-key, but poignant look at the
> racial problem.

Rudyard Kipling, *The Jungle Books*.

> Two volumes. Exciting episodes with jungle animals, written
> with powerful imaginative appeal.

_____, *Just So Stories*.

> Children's animal stories, the only book Kipling illustrated,
> giving amusing answers to questions such as why the leopard
> has spots and where the elephant got his trunk.

Joseph Krumgold, *Onion John*. NM

> Onion John is a simple immigrant vegetable peddler largely
> ignored, but twelve-year-old Andy makes the choice to become
> his friend in spite of social pressure.

_____, *. . . and Now Miguel.* NM
> Miguel wants to join the men who shepherd the sheep in the higher pastures. A tender story about working together and taking responsibility, but also accepting who you are with grace.

Charles and Mary Lamb, *Tales from Shakespeare.*
> A wonderful way to meet Shakespeare. Easy-to-read condensations of the plots, written in good story form.

Andrew Lang, *Red Fairy Book.*
_____, *Blue Fairy Book.*
_____, *Yellow Fairy Book.*
_____, *Green Fairy Book.*
> For those who like fairy tales.

Sidney Lanier, *The Boy's King Arthur,* il. N. C. Wyeth.
> A well-told classic tale. Editions with N. C. Wyeth's illustrations are collector's items.

Robert Lawson, *Rabbit Hill.* NM
> Animal-loving new people move into a run-down house on the hill and good things begin to happen for all the animals.

_____, *A New and Astonishing Life of Ben Franklin as Written by His Very Good Mouse Amos.*
_____, *Mr. Revere and I.*
> An account of certain episodes in Revere's career as told by his horse.

Munro Leaf, *The Story of Ferdinand,* il. Robert Lawson.
> A delightful story of a bull who favored smelling flowers, until the day he went wild from a bee sting just as the men arrived to look for a bull to face the toreador. Read the original.

Lois Lenski, *Strawberry Girl.* NM
> Birdie Boyer is a Florida Cracker whose family raises strawberries in a story full of enterprise and fun and real life.

_____, *Indian Captive: The Story of Mary Jemison.* NM
> Based on the true story of a girl abducted by the Seneca Indians.

Maud H. Lovelace, *Betsy-Tacy,* a series, il. Lois Lenski.
> The story of two young girls, inseparable friends—so close they are regarded as one, and their growing up in a small Minnesota town years ago. Newly back in print.

Betty MacDonald, *Mrs. Piggle-Wiggle,* a series, il. Hilary Knight.

> A remarkable old lady lives in an upside-down house and children love her because she smells of cookies and was once married to a pirate. She also has solutions to almost any problem.

Robert McCloskey, *Homer Price.*

> Homer hits a home run for every reader. The story is funny, inventive, and a wonderful read-aloud book for the family, with the added joy of McCloskey's drawings.

John O'Brien, *Silver Chief: Dog of the North,* il. Kurt Wiese.

> Classic story of a magnificent dog, part husky and part wolf.

Philippa Pearce, *Tom's Midnight Garden.*

> Tom hears the clock strike thirteen one night while staying at his aunt and uncle's apartment. Sleepless and lonely, he goes downstairs to investigate and opens the door, not on the little concrete yard he expects, but on a wonderful garden that takes him back in time. Written in 1958 in England where it was awarded the Carnegie Medal for excellence, this timeless story will probably be reaching out to children in 2102 on both sides of the Atlantic.

Gene Stratton Porter, *A Girl of the Limberlost.*

> Young Elnora Comstock and her difficult mother live deep in the swamplands. Elnora resourcefully and endearingly wades her way through the struggles of poverty, determining to go to high school and overcome her family history.

_____, *Freckles.*

> Freckles, an abandoned armless boy, shows his worth in protecting the valuable timbers of the Limberlost forest and proves that his inner spirit overcomes all other handicaps.

Howard Pyle, *The Story of Sir Lancelot and His Companions.*

_____, *Some Merry Adventures of Robin Hood.*

_____, *Otto of the Silver Hand.*

_____, *The Story of King Arthur and His Knights.*

> Pyle is a delightful storyteller and a splendid artist who greatly influenced Andrew Wyeth. These stories are sure to please boys.

BG/HB	Boston Globe/Horn Book award
CM	Caldecott Medal
CH	Caldecott Honor
CSK	Coretta Scott King award
NA	Newbery Award
NH	Newbery Honor
NM	Newbery Medal

Arthur Ransome, *Swallows and Amazons*.

> The first in a well-loved, irresistible series. Four English children camp on an island and find a world of imagination and unexpected events. Look for *Swallowdale, Peter Duck, Winter Holiday, Coot Club, Pigeon Post*, and others.

Glen Rounds, *The Blind Colt*.

> Born blind, a mustang colt learns to "see" with his ears and nose.

_____, *Paul, the Mighty Logger*.

> Tall tales about Paul Bunyan.

_____, *Whitey Ropes and Rides*.

> A series about Whitey's adventures as a cowhand.

_____, *Hunted Horses*.

> Story about the wild horses of the mesa.
>
> Rounds wrote these stories back in the 1940s; they are still popular with boys.

Felix Salten, *Bambi: A Life in the Woods*.

> A 1926 classic book, to be read to children ten or older. This tender story takes you deep into the forest to know the animals and the precarious life they lead. It is a somber story of wisdom and reality—much more than a Disney cartoon.

Ruth Sawyer, *Roller Skates*. NM

> Freed from her customary restraints when her parents go abroad, a little girl takes readers with her as she explores New York City on roller skates in 1890.

George Selden, *The Cricket in Times Square*, il. Garth Williams.

> A cricket from Connecticut spends the summer in a New York subway station helped by three friends—a boy, a cat, and a fast-talking Broadway mouse.

_____, *Harry Kitten and Tucker Mouse*.

_____, *Tucker's Countryside*.

Kate Seredy, *The Good Master*. NH

> An unforgettable story of a Hungarian tomboy who is sent to live on her uncle's ranch. A marvelous bit of writing from the 1930s.

_____, *The White Stag*. NM

> This story is a vivid portrayal of life on the steppes when the hordes invade. Read this with *The Trumpeter of Krakov* (Eric Kelly) for a well-balanced picture of history.

_____, *The Singing Tree.* NH

> A warm, clear picture of life in pre-World War I Hungary. A
> continuation of *The Good Master*, the farm of the first book
> becomes a refuge for the needy. Kate Seredy's books sing
> with poetic language and vivid descriptions and stay in the
> heart year after year. Read them now; read them when you
> are fifty.

Anna Sewell, *Black Beauty.*

> Moving story of perhaps the most famous horse of all. Don't
> substitute simplified versions for small children.

Monica Shannon, *Dobry.* NM

> Beautifully written story of family life in the mountains of
> Bulgaria, a story to help you see and feel and love. You will
> want it to go on forever.

Armstrong Sperry, *Call It Courage.* NM

> A memorable story of a Polynesian boy who faces his fears and
> a raging sea with courage. A story for boys.

Johanna H. Spyri, *Heidi.*

> An unforgettable story about a girl, her grandfather, and a boy
> named Peter, set in the Swiss mountains. Don't choose a
> simplified edition.

Sydney Taylor, *All-of-a-Kind Family,* a series.

> Ella, Henny, Sara, Charlotte, and Gertie are five lovable
> Jewish girls growing up in New York in the early 1900s—
> an all-of-a-kind family who have immigrated from
> Czechoslovakia. Then baby Charles is born and the fun
> begins.

James Thurber, *Many Moons.* CM

> A princess wants the moon, and the king orders one person
> after another to bring it to her. One succeeds.

_____, *The Thirteen Clocks.*

> The story of a wicked prince who lives in a cold, cold castle
> with the Princess Saralinda where the hands of all the
> clocks are set at ten to five, frozen. Suitors find it hard to
> win the hand of Saralinda, who has the only warm hand in
> the castle.

E. B. White, *Charlotte's Web*, il. Garth Williams.
>   A profound, tender story of a pig and a spider. A classic story of friendship.

_____, *Stuart Little.*
>   Story of the exploits of a brave and debonair mouse.

_____, *The Trumpet of the Swan.*
>   Louis, a voiceless trumpeter swan, learns to play a trumpet and finds fame, fortune, and fatherhood.

Kate Douglas Wiggin, *Rebecca of Sunnybrook Farm.*
>   Irrepressible Rebecca Rowena Randall wins over prim Aunt Miranda, the whole town, and thousands of readers since this book was first published in 1903. An old favorite too good to miss.

Laura Ingalls Wilder, *Little House in the Big Woods*, il. Garth Williams.
>   First of a series of stories about the Ingalls family, full of warmth and the adventure of pioneer days. A must read.

_____, *Little House on the Prairie.*

_____, *Farmer Boy.*

_____, *On the Banks of Plum Creek.*

_____, *By the Shores of Silver Lake.*

_____, *The Long Winter.*

_____, *Little Town on the Prairie.*

_____, *These Happy Golden Years.*

_____, *The First Four Years.*
>   All nine are available in paperback in a slipcase. *Let the Hurricane Roar* by Rose Wilder Lane (Laura's only daughter) is a reprint of a fifty-year-old book available for those who love the Little House books

Johann D. Wyss, *Swiss Family Robinson.*
>   After a shipwreck at sea, the Swiss family find refuge on an island, where they create a new home and way of life. Through difficulties and adventures, their discoveries and ingenuity are inspiring. Read in its original form, this book has a spiritual substance that makes it a splendid and timeless read-aloud for a family. Better still, listen to it read aloud by Books-on-Tape.

Chapter 16

More Great Books for Intermediate Readers: Ages 9–12

Intermediate readers have never had so many books! Here are some favorites for a general listing of books for ages nine to twelve. Simply listing these brings back so many memories of wonderful stories and reading together as a family. Some are new and others are old—not quite classics, but on their way to that list. So many good books strain book lists and excite readers.

I feel new admiration for authors like Lloyd Alexander, who can write a delightfully funny book about a stern aunt who shows a small boy what life is all about (*The Gawgon*), especially after years of immersing himself in fantasy novels that take readers (especially boys) into other worlds. Katherine Paterson is another writer who handles fairy tales and reality with equal skill, capturing in both what is real and important. Her books appeal to both girls and boys.

This listing contains adventure and humor. The age range of nine to twelve is a significant maturity jump. This list has books for both ends of that age spectrum, so look carefully. Have many hours of good reading as you explore this part of the book list.

Karen Ackerman, *Song and Dance Man,* il. Stephen Grammell. CM

> Give Grandpa a copy of this book to read with his eight- or nine-year-old grandchild!

Lloyd Alexander, *The Gawgon.*

> Gawgon (Old Gorgon) is the name given to Aunt Annie who says, "Give me that boy," determined to give David a tutor like none you've ever met. Aunt Annie takes David on unbelievable adventures and fun. This delightful story is a departure from Alexander's tales of heroism in fantasy lands.

_____, *The Iron Ring.*

> Young Tamar, ruler of the small Indian kingdom of Sundari, collects an amusing entourage (his ancient teacher, a cow-tender, a mischievous king of the monkeys, a grumpy eagle) as he returns to Jaya's distant land to make good his debt. Along the way he rescues others, does battle with enemies, and discovers something about the meaning of life. An exciting, agreeable adventure.

John Bibee, *The Mystery of the Homeless Treasure,* a series.

> The detectives are thrown into their first case when they discover a golden teacup stolen thirty years earlier. The first of eight fast-paced mysteries in boxed sets called The Home School Detectives.

Eve Bunting, *The Memory String,* il. Ted Rand.

> The buttons on the memory string that Laura cherishes most belonged to her mother. The most precious of all is one from the nightgown she was wearing when she died three years before. A broken memory string provides an opportunity for Laura to relate with new understanding to a new stepmother.

John Bunyan, *Dangerous Journey,* ed. Oliver Hunkin,
> il. Alan Perry.

> This elaborately illustrated adaptation of *Pilgrim's Progress* is a good way to introduce children to Bunyan's depiction of the Christian journey. Meet memorable characters like Great-Heart, Hopeful, and the Giant of Despair. See what happens in Doubting Castle and the Slough of Despond.

Betsy Byars, *Me Tarzan.*

> Dorothy beats out rival Dwayne for the role of Tarzan in the class play, but discovers her already-stunning yell becomes a genuine primal scream that brings in animals from everywhere, including a nearby circus.

_____, *The Not-Just-Anybody Family.*

> The first in a series of funny tales about the unforgettable Blossom family.

_____, The Disappearing Acts series.

> Herculeah Jones, crime-solver, stars in this series of mystery stories.

_____, *Bingo Brown*, a series.

Ann Cameron, *The Stories Huey Tells,* il. Lis Toft.

> Seven-year-old Huey takes center stage in telling his warmhearted and winsome tales about his family. Like his tag-along dog, Spunky, Huey displays lots of spirit that makes fun reading.

Rebecca Caudill, *Did You Carry the Flag Today, Charley?*

> No one ever expected to see Charley carry the flag because it is an honor given to the most helpful person.

Beverly Cleary, *Henry Huggins,* a series.

> Enjoy the hilarious adventures of Henry, his dog Ribsy, and their friends.

_____, *Ramona's World*, latest in a series of Ramona books.

> Ramona is the most rambunctious eight-year-old you'll ever meet, and she causes her family much frustration. This lovable, energetic little girl will delight readers of all ages with her wit and unusual insights into life.

_____, *Otis Spofford.*

> Otis stirs up a little excitement at school. Brimful of humor.

_____, *Ellen Tebbits.*

> About a fourth grader whose life is made miserable by long underwear.

_____, *Dear Mr. Henshaw*, il. Paul O. Zelinsky. NM

> Sixth-grader Leigh Botts has written letters to Mr. Henshaw since second grade. Now Mr. Henshaw turns and asks the boy questions he struggles to answer.

Andrew Clements, *Frindle*.
> Nick Allen knows how to liven things up at school. He invents a new word for "pen" which begins a hilarious war of words in Mrs. Granger's fifth-grade class.

_____, *The School Story*.
> Aspiring author Natalie decides at age twelve to write a novel, and her friend Zoe, full of plans and chutzpah, sets about to get it published. Both Clements books are fun family read-alouds.

Barbara Cohen, *Thank You, Jackie Robinson*.
> An obsession with the Brooklyn Dodgers cements the friendship of a fatherless boy and an older man. A bittersweet tale of love and loss.

_____, *The Carp in the Bathtub*.
> Leah and her brother try to rescue the carp Momma is keeping in the bathtub to make gefilte fish for Passover.

Christopher Paul Curtis, *Bud, Not Buddy*. NM CSK
> A wonderful story about the durability of the human spirit and the goodness that surrounds desperate little black Bud Caldwell, a runaway from institutional care in the 1930s, who tries to find his father after his mother dies. Humorous, enduring.

_____, *The Watsons Go to Birmingham—1963*. NH CSK
> Ten-year-old Kenny Watson narrates what happens on the family trip from Michigan to Alabama to take his mischief-prone brother Byron to spend the summer with his grandmother. Racism and the Civil Rights Movement rumble in the background of this story, filled with both humor and serious issues.

John D. Fitzgerald, *Great Brain*, a series, il. Mercer Mayer.
> A wonderfully funny story about Tom and his Great Brain, told by his younger brother J. D. The setting is turn-of-the century in Mormon Utah. Your children will want to read them all.

Louise Fitzhugh, *Harriet the Spy*.
> Harriet is not your typical, lovable heroine. In fact, she is an opinionated, nosy brat. Intelligent and curious, Harriet likes to spy on people and write about them in her secret notebook—until she becomes a lonely outcast when others see what she has written. This book has been around a long time and still intrigues kids. Parents sometimes think Harriet a bit brash.

Sid Fleischman, *The Whipping Boy,* il. Peter Sis. NM

> The adventures of a spoiled young prince and the "whipping boy" who had been brought to the palace to take all the prince's punishments for him. When they escape together, the prince learns about loyalty and courage from his new friend.

Doris Gates, *Blue Willow.* NM

> The tender story of a daughter of migrant farm workers who wishes for a permanent home and keeps a blue willow plate to remind her of a former way of life.

Jean Craighead George, *My Side of the Mountain.*

> A contemporary Robinson Crusoe—a small boy learns to survive and live with nature in the Catskills.

_____, *Julie of the Wolves.* NM

> Miyax, a young Eskimo girl, gets lost without compass or food. Slowly a pack of Arctic wolves begin to care for her and she learns to live with them.

_____, *Water Sky.*

> Nothing in young Lincoln's past prepares him for whaling camp on the Arctic waters off Barrow, where he meets young Eskimos and finds more than the uncle he is looking for. George's books have an environmental emphasis.

William Goldman, *The Princess Bride: S. Morgenstern's Classic Tale of True Love and High Adventure.*

> The most beautiful girl marries the handsomest man and he turns out not to be the man of her dreams. This is fantasy with hilarious reality. The movie caught the basic story line, but the book sets out to prove that life isn't fair.

Kevin Henkes, *Sun and Spoon.*

> Spoon Gilmore takes the deck of solitaire cards as a keepsake to remember his grandmother after her death. Later, his grandfather shares his own sentimental attachment to those same cards. As he talks Spoon begins to see what made his grandparents' relationship so special.

Russell Hoban, *The Mouse and His Child,* il. David Small.

> A serious book which addresses some of the sadder parts of life, but also deals with the transforming power of love. A highly praised book that past readers are glad to see reissued. Eleven and up.

_____, *How Tom Beat Captain Najork and His Hired Sportsmen*,
   il. Quentin Blake.

> This book begins with a giggle and ends with a giggle, but
> in between it is the story of Tom, a tiny boy, with a flair for
> fooling around, and whose formidable Aunt Fidget decides
> to put a stop to it.

Holling Clancy Holling, *Paddle to the Sea.*

> A modern classic of a little carved Indian-in-a-canoe that floats
> through the Great Lakes and on to the sea with the help of
> many people along the way. Holling is a master at weaving
> history, geography, and other enlightening details, both with
> words and pictures, into a thoroughly engaging tale.

_____, *Minn of Mississippi.*

> Minn, a three-legged snapping turtle, travels from the
> headwaters to the mouth of the Mississippi River.

_____, *Pagoo.*

> The life story of a hermit crab. Holling's books appeal to a
> wide age range (fathers would enjoy!) and are great additions
> to a library.

Polly Hovarth, *The Trolls.*

> Aunt Sally comes to baby-sit at the last minute so the parents
> can take a trip, and brings family history to the Anderson
> children. She tells hilarious story after story, but one that is
> not so funny teaches the children to value their family.

Dick King-Smith, *Mysterious Miss Slade.*

> When Patsy and Jim Reader move into an English cottage they
> befriend reclusive Miss Slade, who lives with a malodorous
> ménage of animals, thinking she needs help. Miss Slade proves
> to be the wealthy Honorable Margaretta Slade who only
> needs some friendship to draw her out of her more deleterious
> idiosyncrasies. With King-Smith's brisk sense of humor, readers
> will have fun.

**E. L. Konigsburg, *From the Mixed-Up Files of Mrs. Basil E.
   Frankweiler.* NM**

> Two children run away to live in the Metropolitan Museum
> of Art and find a mysterious sculpture, artist unknown. They
> set about to search through the files of Mrs. B. Frankweiler
> to discover the truth.

_____, *The View from Saturday.* NM

> Four students on the sixth-grade quiz team call themselves "The Souls" (one of the closest friendships in history!). As they win more and more competitions, they also teach their handicapped coach about love and friendship.

Jane Kurtz, *Jakarta Missing.*

> Twelve-year-old Dakar has trouble adjusting to her family's move from Kenya to North Dakota, especially since they leave her beautiful sister Jakarta behind in boarding school. Eventually trouble forces Jakarta to return home. Almost everything in Cottonwood, North Dakota requires bravery for girls who have grown up in Africa, who learn that life is both terrifying and wonderful. A good story to help children who have never moved to appreciate cultural change. Eleven and up.

_____, *I'm Sorry, Almira Ann*, il. Susan Havice.

> A story about the friendship of two girls moving westward on an Oregon wagon train.

Astrid Lindgren, *Pippi Longstocking,* a series.

> Pippi lives alone except for her monkey, her horse, and her fortune in gold pieces, but she creates a sensation wherever her hilarious adventures take her. Just right stories for fourth graders.

Patricia MacLachlan, *Sarah, Plain and Tall.* NM

> Anna and Caleb's widowed father corresponds with a mail-order bride from Maine and invites her to come for a visit. She replies, "I will come by train. I will wear a yellow bonnet. I am plain and tall."

_____, *Skylark.*

_____, *Caleb.*

> Both books continue the story of Anna and Caleb's family.

_____, *The Facts and Fictions of Minna Pratt.*

> A story that sparkles with humor, elegant prose, and superb storytelling. Eleven-year-old Minna Pratt is brimful of wishes and impatience with her family and her "vibrato."

_____, *Baby.*

> Two troubled families are healed when their paths join and a year-old baby is left on the Larkin's porch. A story that lingers in the heart.

_____, *Journey.*

BG/HB	Boston Globe/Horn Book award
CM	Caldecott Medal
CH	Caldecott Honor
CSK	Coretta Scott King award
NA	Newbery Award
NH	Newbery Honor
NM	Newbery Medal

Walt Morey, *Death Walk.*
>   Joel Rogers fights for his life alone and injured in the Alaskan
>   wilderness until he is rescued by a mysterious trapper.

_____, *Canyon Winter.*
>   Peter survives a private plane crash and learns to survive from
>   the rough and unforgiving Omar Pickett. A story reminiscent
>   of Gary Paulsen's *Hatchet.*

_____, *Gentle Ben.*
>   The lonely son of a salmon fisherman befriends an Alaskan
>   brown bear that has been mistreated.

_____, *Gloomy Gus.*
>   A bear cub and a lonely boy in Alaska whose father says the pet
>   bear must go.

_____, *Kavik the Wolf Dog.*

Susie Morgenstern, *A Book of Coupons,* il. Serge Bloch.
>   Their new fifth-grade teacher is like Santa Claus, his students
>   think, but then find out that the real gift he gives is a love
>   of learning. Steig-like drawings, humorous. Translated from
>   French.

Ursula Nordstrom, *The Secret Language.*
>   Boarding school turned out even worse than Victoria North,
>   age eight, expected, until her quirky classmate Martha Sherman
>   took her under her wing and into a magical world of secret
>   language.

Scott O'Dell, *Island of the Blue Dolphins.* NM
>   Haunting story, based on fact, of an Indian girl who is forced
>   to spend eighteen years alone on an island off the coast of
>   California where she must rely on her own skills. *Zia* is a
>   sequel.

_____, *Black Star, Bright Dawn.*
>   Bright Dawn is an Eskimo girl who is rescued by her favorite
>   dog on an incredibly difficult sled-dog race of nearly 1200
>   miles. A fine novel.

_____, *Sing Down the Moon.*
>   A first-person narrative of a fourteen-year-old Navajo girl on
>   the long walk when her tribe was forced out of Arizona and
>   sent to New Mexico.

_____, *The Road to Damietta.*

_____, *The Serpent Never Sleeps.*
>   O'Dell is a marvelous writer whose strong characters model
>   good things for readers.

Katherine Paterson, *The King's Equal,* il. Vladimir Vagin.
>   This book is available as a picture book, or as a chapter book.
>   Raphael cannot be crowned king until he marries someone who
>   is his equal, an unlikely situation since Raphael already thinks
>   he is the best. Many questions pour out of the pages of this
>   book, discussed in chapter 4.

_____, *The Wide Awake Princess*, il. Vladimir Vagin.
_____, *Celia and the Sweet Water,* il. Vladimir Vagin.
_____, *The Bridge to Terabithia.* NM
_____, *The Great Gilly Hopkins.*

Robert Newton Peck, *A Day No Pigs Would Die.*
>   A poignant story taken from Peck's childhood, his relationship
>   to his father, and his coming to terms with his father's work.
>   A story of life and death, this is a book to talk about together.

_____, *A Part of the Sky*, a sequel.

Barbara Robinson, *My Brother Louis Measures Worms.*
>   One of ten interconnected stories about the Lawsons, an
>   ordinary family with just a few hilarious eccentricities.

_____, *The Best Christmas Pageant Ever.*
>   An annual favorite in which the rowdy Herdman family takes
>   over the church Christmas pageant.

Alfred Slote, *Finding Buck Henry.*
>   Jason, an eleven-year-old Little League player, makes a startling
>   connection while he is looking up his heroes in a baseball card
>   shop. Is Buck Henry, the famous pitcher of the Negro League,
>   the school custodian whose name is Mack Henry?

Jerry Spinelli, *Maniac Magee.* NM
>   Young Jeffrey Magee loses his parents early in life and heads off
>   on his own. Soon he discovers a small town where he adopts
>   various families and teaches some surprising lessons about racism.

_____, *Crash.*
>   A budding football star learns some valuable things about life
>   when a new neighbor moves in next door. A touching book
>   about life, death, and the way we treat others.

_____, *Stargirl*.

> Stargirl (otherwise known as Susan) marches to a different drummer, which alternately draws people to her or makes them shun her. Leo tries to persuade her to conform, but it doesn't work. Spinelli paints Stargirl larger than life to offer a winsome commentary on conformity.

Patricia St. John, *Where the River Begins*.

> A contemporary story about a boy named Francis, who comes from a troubled family. He gets involved with a street gang, and in desperation goes to live with a farm family who had earlier befriended him.

_____, *Star of Light*.

> Hamid lives in a mountain village in Morocco. He saves his little blind sister from being sold as a beggar. All ages.

_____, *Treasures of the Snow*.

> A skiing accident teaches a class of Swiss children about caring for each other.

_____, *Runaway*.

_____, *The Tanglewood's Secrets*.

_____, *The Secret at Pheasant Cottage*.

> All St. John's books have a fine spiritual tone.

Joni Eareckson Tada, Darcy and Friends series.

> Darcy is a sixth grader in a bright purple wheelchair, facing junior high school and the challenges of her handicap. Written by a woman who was paralyzed as a teen in a diving accident.

Theodore Taylor, *The Cay*.

> Shipwrecked on a deserted island (a cay), a young boy and an old man named Timothy must learn to survive the elements and each other.

_____, *Timothy of the Cay*, a prequel.

Jane Yolen, Robert J. Harris, *Queen's Own Fool*,
> il. Cynthia von Buhler.

> In 1559 thirteen-year-old Nicola Ambruzzi, a member of a ragtag troupe of entertainers in the French court, impresses the young Queen Mary with her wit and honesty. She takes the girl under her protection as "the Queen's own fool," commanding her to speak the truth boldly in an atmosphere of schemes and fawning lies.

Chapter 17

Stories for Animal Lovers: Ages 9–12

Children go on reading binges about certain subjects. Animal stories is one of the favorite categories. Some of these stories are funny; others touch the heart and bring tears. But all of them teach children about courage and love.

William H. Armstrong, *Sounder*. NM

The heart-wrenching story of a great coon dog and his black master.

Michael Bond, *A Bear Called Paddington*, il. Peggy Fortrum.

A series about a bear, traveling from Peru, who is found in the London train station. Paddington lives on the edge of disaster and emerges triumphant.

Sheila Burnford, *The Incredible Journey*.

Journey of a Siamese cat, an English bull terrier, and a Labrador retriever. It's been made into a movie, but don't let that keep you from reading it aloud.

Kate DiCamillo, *Because of Winn-Dixie*.

India Opal Buloni (called Opal) thinks life is "sweetness and sadness all mixed-up together." When she finds a ragged stray dog in the supermarket, she adopts him and names him after the store, Winn-Dixie. His friendly manner wins over her father, and the dog begins to help Opal overcome her problems in making friends in a new place. A sweet, funny story.

Walter Farley, *Black Stallion*, il. Domenick D'Andrea.

This story of a wild Arabian stallion and the boy who trained him still pleases readers. Many other books follow in the series written in 1941.

John Reynolds Gardiner, *Stone Fox*.

Little Willy is out to save Grandfather's farm by entering his beloved dog, Searchlight, in a dogsled race against the legendary "Stone Fox" and his five experienced sled dogs. A touching story about the value of persistence.

Fred Gipson, *Old Yeller*.

When a big, mud-splattered yellow dog shows up at Travis's house, he thinks the dog is an awful coward, but when a bear attacks Travis's younger brother, "Old Yeller" saves his life. His tender friendship with this dog ends with one of the hardest things Travis will ever need to do.

Marguerite Henry, ***King of the Wind,*** **il. Wesley Dennis. NM**
> The unforgettable story of Agba, the stable boy and the golden-red stallion born of the Sultan of Morocco's stable with a white spot on his heel, a symbol of speed.

_____, *Misty of Chincoteague.*

_____, *Sea Star.*

_____, *Stormy, Misty's Foal.*

_____, *Born to Trot.*
> Henry is considered by many to be the best writer of horse stories.

Will James, ***Smoky: The Cow Horse.*** **NM**
> Written in cowboy vernacular, this is a powerful book. If children are going to weep over animal stories, here is one worth their tears.

Dick King-Smith, ***The School Mouse.***
> Mice generally don't read, but Flora, who lives in a school cupboard, wants to learn the same things the human children learn. She learns enough reading to save her family's life when exterminators set out tantalizing (but clearly labeled) rodent poison around the school.

_____, *The Water Horse.*

_____, *Babe, the Gallant Pig.*

_____, *Lady Lollipop.*

_____, *Spider Sparrow.*
> King-Smith's animal stories are great family read-alouds.

James A. Kjelgaard, ***Big Red.***
> From the moment he sees the beautiful champion Irish setter, Danny knows this is the dog for him. Together they face dangers in the harsh Wintapi wilderness and have their courage tested by the undisputed king of the wilderness—the bear.

_____, *Irish Red: Son of Big Red.*

_____, *Outlaw Red.*

_____, *Stormy.*

_____, *Snow Dog.*
> Kjelgaard and his dog stories are hard to beat.

Eric Knight, ***Lassie Come Home.***
> Get the original classic dog story written in 1938. It's the best!

Jack London, *Call of the Wild.*

Buck, stolen from his comfortable home in California, must learn the hardships of being a sled dog in the Yukon. In this hostile environment he becomes a truly heroic dog.

Farley Mowat, *Owls in the Family.*

Memories of growing up in northern Saskatchewan, Canada, with lots of family pets—including two comical owls. A hilarious boyhood tale.

Illustration by N. C. Wyeth reprinted with the permission of Charles Scribner's Sons from *The Yearling* by Marjorie Kinnan Rawlings. Copyright 1939 by Charles Scribner's Sons.

Phyllis Reynolds Naylor, *Shiloh,* a trilogy. NM

> Marty Preston rescues a mistreated beagle, but faces complex
> ethical problems. Should he return the beagle to its owner for
> more cruel treatment? He decides to hide it, which involves
> lying and stealing food from the table. The story and its two
> sequels handles his love affair with this dog and solving his
> dilemma.

_____, *Saving Shiloh.*

_____, *Shiloh Season.*

Sterling North, *Rascal.*

> An autobiographical account of the beauty of nature as
> experienced by an eleven-year-old and his sometimes comical
> pet raccoon.

Mary O'Hara, *My Friend Flicka.*

> Having Flicka for his own helps a dreamy and lonely boy grow
> up to meet his father's expectations. An emotional book, it's a
> story that Americans, young and old, have taken to their hearts.

_____, *Thunderhead.*

_____, *The Catch Colt.*

Marjorie Rawlings, *The Yearling,* il. N. C. Wyeth. Pulitzer Prize.

> Living in the scrublands of Florida with his family, Jody Baxter
> finds a beautiful fawn, makes him a pet, and names him Flag.
> What follows is a year of hard decisions and courage. Written
> for adults, but appropriated by children. Look for the edition
> with Wyeth's superb illustrations.

Wilson Rawls, *Where the Red Fern Grows.*

> Billy wants a pair of coon hounds more than anything, but has
> no money. How Billy gets the dogs and what they mean to him
> is the theme of this story. A wonderful, teary-eyed book to talk
> about with someone else.

John Steinbeck, *The Red Pony.*

> When his pony dies, John discovers the meaning of life.

Robbyn Smith van Frankenhuyzen, *Adopted by an Owl,* il.
Gijsbert van Frankenhuyzen.

> A fine, true story of Jackson the owl, with spectacular
> illustrations!

Chapter 18

Historical Novels: Ages 9–12

Historical novels are surely the most entertaining way to acquaint children with history. History is not a dull subject, because it is filled with characters very much like the people we meet in stories. Historical novels are based on historical facts, and then embroidered with fictional events and people.

Many of these make wonderful read-aloud stories for families to enjoy together because they hold the attention of a wide age-range.

Jennifer Armstrong, *Shipwreck at the Bottom of the World: The Extraordinary True Story of Shackleton and the Endurance.*

The harrowing survival story of English explorer Sir Ernest Shackleton and the ill-fated *Endurance*. As Shackleton and twenty-seven sailors attempted to cross the frozen Antarctic continent, they faced being trapped in an ice pack, losing their ship, surviving winter, and being attacked by sea lions. The story, told by a young stowaway on the *Endurance*, is a compelling adventure, well told. Eleven and up.

Mary Jane Auch, *Journey to Nowhere.*
_____, *Frozen Summer.*
_____, *The Road to Home.*

In this trilogy, Remembrance Nye (Mem), motherless and thirteen, assumes the care of her younger brother and sister as her father becomes increasingly irresponsible, essentially abandoning them when he goes to work on the Erie Canal. Mem resolves to continue on with her siblings to find relatives in Connecticut, a journey on which she is alternately cheated and helped. Set in 1817, the stories are a historical slice of life.

Patricia Beatty, *Turn Homeward, Hannalee.*
_____, *Be Ever Hopeful, Hannalee.*

Hannalee has been sent to work in a mill in Indiana during the Civil War and now tries to return to find her family in war-torn Georgia. In the sequel, the family returns to devastated Atlanta in the summer of 1865.

Joan W. Blos, *A Gathering of Days.* NM

A fictional journal of Catherine, a young New England girl, in about 1830. The help she offers a runaway slave brings her some growing-up grief.
_____, *Brothers of the Heart.*

In the 1830s Shem, a fourteen-year-old crippled boy, leaves his wilderness home after a series of misunderstandings and is eventually helped by an old Indian woman.

Rhoda Blumberg, *Commodore Perry in the Land of the Shogun.*

Historical fiction about Matthew Perry's adventurous expedition to open Japan to American trade, a task complicated

by cultural differences that make understanding and trust
difficult.

_____, *Shipwrecked!*

The true tale of Manjiro who, after being shipwrecked in 1841
off the coast of his native Japan, was rescued by an American
whaling ship. He was subsequently educated in New England
and returned home to become an honored samurai. Both books
are good ways to acquaint young readers with cross-cultural
understanding.

**Robert Burleigh, *Black Whiteness: Admiral Byrd Alone in the
Antarctic,*** il. Walter Lyon Krudop.

A retelling of Admiral Richard Byrd's successful one-man
Antarctic encampment, a story of his determination and
courage. A great adventure story for boys.

Joan Dash, *The World at Her Fingertips: The Story of Helen Keller.*

A wonderfully told story of a determined, obstinate woman
who was extraordinarily dependent, despite her drive for
independence. Inspiring.

Walter D. Edmonds, *The Matchlock Gun.* NM

In 1756, New York was a British colony with French-Indian
uprisings a constant threat to Edward and his family. When his
father is called away, Edward is left to protect his mother and
little Trudy. Based on a true story.

Russell Freedman, *Out of Darkness: The Story of Louis Braille,*
il. Kate Kiesler.

Over 170 years ago a blind fifteen-year-old French boy
developed a system of raised paper punches that would enable
a blind person to read.

_____, *Give Me Liberty: The Story of the Declaration of Independence.*
The night of the Boston Tea Party, a fourteen-year-old sneaks
aboard the ships in the harbor. Freedman is a master at taking
crucial moments in American history and reproducing them
with powerful tensions and grace.

_____, *The Wright Brothers: How They Built the Airplane.*

_____, *Eleanor Roosevelt: A Life of Discovery.*

_____, *The Life and Death of Crazy Horse.*

Jean Fritz, *George Washington's Breakfast.*
_____, *What's the Big Idea, Ben Franklin?*
_____, *Shh! We're Writing the Constitution.*
_____, *Where Was Patrick Henry on the 29th of May?*
_____, *Why Don't You Get a Horse, Sam Adams?*

> Looking at titles like these (and many more), you already know that Fritz will teach your children history in the most palatable way.

James Cross Giblin, *The Amazing Life of Benjamin Franklin,*
il. Michael Dooling.

> Did you know Ben Franklin's son remained loyal to England during the War of Independence? Born in Boston to a family of seventeen children, apprenticed to his brother, a printer—Ben could be called a world statesman, inventor, politician, but by his own choice, his gravestone reads simply B. Franklin, Printer.

_____, *George Washington.*
_____, *Thomas Jefferson.*
_____, *Charles Lindbergh.*
_____, *Fireworks, Picnics, and Flags,* il. Ursula Arndt.

> A wonderful family book about the origins of Independence Day and symbols, from the flag to the story behind America's most famous patriotic bald eagle to Uncle Sam.

Sheila Gordon, *Waiting for the Rain: A Novel of South Africa.*

> The story of two boys—one white, the other black—and their close friendship in the tensions of apartheid.

Anne Holm, *North to Freedom.*

> A boy who has grown up in a concentration camp makes his way across Europe alone, hoping to find his mother at the end of the journey. A wonderful story.

Gloria Houston, *Bright Freedom's Song: A Story of the Underground Railroad.*

> Bright Freedom Cameron finds out where her name comes from as she learns the history of indentured white people and becomes involved in her family's part in rescuing runaway slaves about the time of the Civil War. Informative and inspiring. A good family read-aloud. Compare this book with Mary Stolz's *Cezanne Pinto* and Roni Schlotter's *F is for Freedom.*

Judith Kerr, *When Hitler Stole Pink Rabbit.*

> Story of a Jewish German refugee family who escaped to Switzerland to avoid Nazi persecution. Ennobling because it shows that people can live happy lives, even amid insecurity and deprivation, if they have the support of a loving family.

Jean Lee Latham, *Carry On, Mr. Bowditch.* NM

> Fictionalized biography about Nat Bowditch who in the late 1700s was sold to a Ship Chandler as an indentured servant for nine years.

Milton Meltzer, *Mary McLeod Bethune: Voice of Black Hope,* il. Stephen Marcheis.

> The first of her family to be born free of slavery, Mary Bethune opens a school for five black girls in 1904 and goes on to become an influential civil rights leader.

Joan Lowry Nixon, *A Family Apart: The Orphan Train Quartet.*

> A series of books about the Kelly children whose penniless mother must send them west on an orphan train in 1860.

Scott O'Dell, *The Hawk That Dare Not Hunt by Day.*

> Set in the time of Tyndale's translation of the Bible into English, Tom Barton and his Uncle Jack, a smuggler, are caught up in Tyndale's problems.

_____, *The King's Fifth.*

> The hero is a young Spanish mapmaker traveling with the conquistadors in southwest America looking for gold.

_____, *Streams to the River, River to the Sea: A Novel of Sacagawea.*

> O'Dell tells the story as though it were written by Sacagawea, skillfully recreating the exploration of Lewis and Clark.

_____, *Sarah Bishop.*

> Based on an actual historical event, Sarah takes refuge in a cave after her father and brother are killed in the Revolutionary War. A good read-aloud.

Dorothy Sterling, *Freedom Train.*

> Story of Harriet Tubman, the courageous escaped slave who devoted her life to helping others escape.

Rosemary Sutcliff, *Sword Song*.

> A young Viking warrior, Bjarni Sigurdson, is barely sixteen when he is banished from his settlement on the west coast of Scotland for accidentally killing a man. He sets out to make a life for himself as a swordsman, finds a hero in a Viking seafarer, and proves himself in five years of adventures. A fine book about difficult choices that lead to maturity.

_____, *Warrior Scarlet*.

> In Bronze Age Britain young Drem, who has a withered arm, must overcome his disability to prove his manhood and become a warrior.

_____, *Black Ships Before Troy: The Story of the Iliad*, il. Alan Lee.

_____, *The Wanderings of Odysseus: The Story of the Odyssey*,
> il. Alan Lee.

> Rosemary Sutcliff breathes life into history. Look for her other titles.

Tomas Szabo, *Boy on the Rooftop*.

> Story about the Hungarian revolution and escape to the West. Exciting reading, especially for early teens who read with difficulty.

Elizabeth Van Steenwyk, *A Traitor Among Us*.

> In the fall of 1944 in Nazi-occupied Holland, thirteen-year-old Pieter knows there is a traitor in the village. Who is it?

Gloria Whelan, *Angel on the Square*.

> Katya Ivanova, daughter of the lady-in-waiting in the Tsars palace, lives an aristocratic life in St. Petersburg in 1914 as the flame of the Russian Revolution ignites.

_____, *Once on This Island*.

_____, *Farewell to the Island*.

_____, *Return to the Island*.

> A series of three stories about life on Mackinac Island during the War of 1812 when the British take over the island from the Americans.

Chapter 19

Fantasy Novels: Ages 9–12

Fantasy novels tell us that there is more to the world than we presently see. As people who truly believe this, Christians are among those most interested in fantasy. Fantasy stands apart from our experience, but it is *about* our experience. It's about another time and place. That's why we like the formula, "Once upon a time in a far-off land . . ." This makes us listen and look more carefully, and as we do we find truth exposed in new ways.

A writer may have difficulty creating heroes and nobility out of the stuff our present world offers. In fantasy one can have transcendence, deity, glory, heroism, courage, goodness, and beauty in a huge universe that shows us truths we cannot see in our smaller world. This allows fantasies to present more philosophical thoughts than we get in most contemporary novels.

Not all fantasies live up to this noble description, but the potential is there, especially as readers grow older and encounter more complicated stories. It makes a good genre to explore.

Lynne Reid Banks, *The Indian in the Cupboard.*

> With a twist of a key in the cupboard, Omri turns small plastic figures into vigorous life and adventure. Captivating battles take place; the quirks in the characters complicate predicaments.

_____, *The Return of the Indian*, a sequel.

_____, *I, Houdini*.

> The amazing story of an escape-artist hamster.

James Barrie, *Peter Pan*, il. Nora S. Unwin.

> Familiar story of a boy who doesn't want to grow up. Read it as it was originally written if you want to meet Barrie's Peter Pan.

L. Frank Baum, *The Wizard of Oz*.

> Made popular by a movie, this book written in 1900 gives a different experience than the film. Meet Dorothy, the Tin Man, the Cowardly Lion, Toto, and the rest.

John Bibee, *The Magic Bicycle*.

> The first of eight books in The Spirit Flyer series. The ordinary town of Centerville is the setting for some extraordinary events. When several children discover that Spirit Flyer bicycles possess strange and magical powers, they are thrust into a conflict with Goliath Industries—with the fate of the town in balance. Allegorical adventure.

_____, *The Toy Campaign*.

_____, *The Only Game in Town* and others in the series.

L. M. Boston, *The Children of Green Knowe*.

_____, *Treasure of Green Knowe*.

_____, *Enemy at Green Knowe*.

_____, *The River at Green Knowe*.

_____, *A Stranger at Green Knowe*.

_____, *The Stone of Green Knowe*.

> English fantasy, beautifully written and completely absorbing. A lonely child is sent to live with his great-grandmother at the family's ancient manor house, Green Knowe.

Lewis Carroll, *Alice's Adventures in Wonderland and Through the Looking Glass*.

> An absolutely ageless classic of fanciful nonsense and satire. A must for every child—and adult. I like the edition illustrated by Helen Oxenbury.

John Christopher, *The White Mountains.*

_____, *The City of Gold and Lead.*

_____, *The Pool of Fire.*

> A compelling science-fiction trilogy about Tripods, huge three-legged machines that descend to earth and take control of people.

Carlo Collodi, *Adventures of Pinocchio.*

> The story of a carver and his boy. An old favorite that needs to be read in the original version.

Ian Fleming, *Chitty-Chitty Bang-Bang,* il. John Burningham.

> A special thirtieth anniversary edition of a magical racing car that flies, floats, and has a real talent for getting the Pott family in and out of trouble. Written by the same man who wrote the James Bond novels.

Kenneth Grahame, *The Wind in the Willows,* il. Ernest Shepard.

> A wonderful, unforgettable tale of beloved Mole, Rat, Badger, and Toad in their classic adventures. Often read too young. Ageless.

_____, *The Reluctant Dragon.*

> Tale of a dragon who prefers poetry to battle.

Brian Jacques, *Redwall,* a series.

> Many teens (and younger) have bookshelves lined with fourteen or more Redwall series books. These inspiring stories of heroism, bravery, and integrity involve an abbey called Redwall where a colony of brave mice live. Subsequent volumes have battles and mysteries and adventures enough to grab a wide age-range of readers. I like them and so do my middle school friends. Look for *Mossflower, Mattimeo, Mariel of Redwall,* and others.

_____, *Castaways of the Flying Dutchman.*

> The legend of the never-ending voyage of a fatal ship begins the story. Neb, a young boy serving as cook's helper, and his dog Denmark are washed safely ashore, are blessed by an angel, and begin an eternal journey to accomplish good works wherever they go.

Norton Juster, *The Phantom Tollbooth,* il. Jules Feiffer.

> "It leaps, soars, and abounds with the right notes all over the place," writes Maurice Sendak in the preface of the thirty-fifth

anniversary edition of this witty novel. A bored boy finds a phantom tollbooth in his room and his adventures begin. It's a must that your children visit the town of Doldrums and climb the Mountain of Ignorance and meet the two princesses named Rhyme and Reason and all the other fantastical places in this story.

Madeline L'Engle, *A Wrinkle in Time*. NM
_____, *A Wind in the Door.*
_____, *A Swiftly Tilting Planet.*
> Interplanetary suspense and adventure in a fantasy trilogy. In the first story three young people go on a dangerous quest to free their father from captivity in another world. Conflict between good and evil explicit in the stories.

C. S. Lewis, The Chronicles of Narnia.
> Lewis believed any book worth reading at ten should be worth reading at fifty, and he wrote that kind—ageless. The series includes: *The Lion, the Witch, and the Wardrobe; Prince Caspian; Voyage of the Dawn Treader; The Silver Chair; The Horse and His Boy; The Magician's Nephew;* and *The Last Battle.* Every child ought to hear these read aloud over and over, and then to read them again and again, since adults enjoy them as much as children. The deeper meaning is significant.

George MacDonald, *At the Back of the North Wind.*
> Classic fantasy with deeper meanings to think about. Diamond has a special friendship with the North Wind, who shows him the world as she sees it.

_____, *The Princess and the Goblin.*
> A princess and a miner's son outwit the evil mountain goblins.

_____, *The Princess and Curdie* is a wonderful sequel.
_____, *The Light Princess.*
> The princess has no gravity and thus cannot participate in life in her world.

A. A. Milne, *Winnie-the-Pooh*, il. E. H. Shepard.
_____, *The House at Pooh Corner.*
> This lovable bear and his friends—Piglet, Tigger, Owl, Roo, Kanga, and Eeyore—are certain to delight every Christopher Robin, regardless of age. Readers will recognize people they know in the characters.

Edith Nesbit, *Five Children and It,* a series.
> Digging in the sand, the children discover a long-missing sand fairy, and the discovery both enlivens and confuses their lives. Written in 1902, this is still a winner.

_____, *The Story of the Treasure Seekers.*

_____, *The Story of the Amulet.*

Mary Norton, *The Borrowers,* a series, il. Beth and Joe Krush. CM
> Tiny people, no taller than a pencil, live in old houses and borrow what they need from whoever lives there. Favorites with readers for many years.

J. K. Rowling, *Harry Potter and the Sorcerer's Stone.*
> Harry Potter, in a captivating and imaginative series (eventually it will be seven books), has taken young readers by storm. Rowling creates a parallel world to Muggles (ordinary humans) in a School for Wizards to which Harry Potter is sent. Together with his friends Ron and Hermione, Harry explores the secret of the sorcerer's stone, fights against evil forces, learns the consequences of choices, and generally has enough adventures to make up many magical books. Children ages eight and older are eager readers of books 1–3. Harry Potter is eleven when the story begins, but with each book he is a year older and the plot becomes darker and more complicated. Books 5–7 are not in print at this writing, but books 4–7 may be best for readers twelve and older. Parents could profitably read these books with their kids.

Antoine de Saint Exupery, *The Little Prince.*
> This wise, enchanting tale chronicles the events following the author's plane crash in the Sahara Desert. There he meets an extraordinary small person who tells a remarkable story about the planet he came from and his quest for what is really important in life. Now in a sixtieth anniversary edition, this book has been translated into more languages than any other book, except the Bible. Age twelve and up.

Pamela Travers, *Mary Poppins,* a series.
> Mary Poppins blew in with the east wind to be nurse for the Banks children. Do read the original version of these! The film version is delightful, but it does not have Pamela Travers' Mary Poppins.

John White, *The Tower of Geburah*.

Book three in the Archives of Anthropos series. In these stories, written in the tradition of the Narnia books, three children enter another land in another time. In an exciting, imaginative story line, the children get involved in the massive struggle between the forces of good and evil. Now a sixth book, *The Dark Lord's Demise*, has been published to end the series.

Drawing by E. H. Shepard from *Winnie-the-Pooh*
by A. A. Milne. Copyright © 1956 by A. A. Milne.
Reproduced by permission of the publishers.

Young Adult Novels: Ages 12–14

Putting ages on books is difficult at best. Some of these books will be consumed by ages eleven and twelve, while others won't have much appeal before fourteen. An expanded list, with more detail, is found in *Honey for a Teen's Heart*.

Adults enjoy these books as much as young teens. One of the great things about being a parent is that you get to catch up on what you missed. Happy reading.

Joan Aiken, *The Wolves of Willoughby Chase.*
_____, *Nightbirds on Nantucket.*
_____, *Black Hearts in Battersea.*

> In a great English estate surrounded by hungry wolves, two girls are mistakenly left in the care of a wicked governess. Stories of adventure, romance, and melodrama. Incredible characters are encountered in these Gothic thrillers.

_____, *The Stolen Lake.*
_____, *Go Saddle the Sea.*
_____, *Bridle the Wind.*
_____, *The Teeth of the Gale.*

Lloyd Alexander, Chronicles of Prydain.

> Excellent fantasy, well written, and based on Welsh legend, the Chronicles include the first five books listed.

_____, *The Book of Three.*
_____, *The Black Cauldron.*
_____, *The Castle of Llyr.*
_____, *Taran Wanderer.*
_____, *The High King.*
_____, *The Westmark Trilogy.*
_____, *The Illyrian Adventure.*
_____, *Gypsy Rizka.*

Mabel Esther Allan, *A Lovely Tomorrow.*

> Frue Allan, a teen growing up in London, is suddenly robbed of her home, parents, and future acting career when a rocket hits her city home on New Year's Eve 1944. She is packed away with her great-aunt far out in the country, and then enrolled in a boarding school where conditions are less than luxurious. Despite these difficulties, Frue eventually finds friendship, love, and even romance in her country home.

Avi, *The True Confessions of Charlotte Doyle.*

> In 1832, resourceful thirteen-year-old Charlotte is the only female on a sailing vessel bound from England to Rhode Island, and is drawn into the adventure and almost-mutiny on the ship. It's a ripping good tale in spite of many questions about how likely it is that a girl could get away with this.

_____, *Nothing But the Truth: A Documentary Novel.*

> The struggles of freshman Philip Malloy and his antipathy towards his teacher let readers look and learn some practical lessons about being a growing person.

_____, *The Secret School.*

> When Mr. Jordan, head of the school board, refuses to hire a replacement teacher for the small one-room rural school in Colorado, resourceful fourteen-year-old Ida Bidson takes over the school as her only chance to graduate and go on to high school.

Natalie Babbitt, *Tuck Everlasting.*

> A girl of ten is befriended by a family that has drunk at a spring that gives them eternal life—and eternal life proves to be a burden. This may seem too juvenile for this classification but the book requires more thoughtful analysis than a younger person would give it. Adults enjoy this story. A good book for discussion.

Margot Benary-Isbert, *A Time to Love.*

> A young German girl and her Great Dane are sent away to a private boarding school during World War II. At Heilingwald she develops her love for music, meets her first love, and learns some valuable lessons about life and its heartaches.

Beverly Butler, *Light a Single Candle.*

> At fourteen Cathy Wheeler loses her sight and is plunged into a world of changes and new experiences. She and her guide dog Trudy are enrolled in Burton Academy for the Blind. Learning Braille, acquiring new independence, and making valuable friends all help Cathy before she accepts the challenge of going back to public high school.

Betsy Byars, *The Summer of the Swans.* NM

> A tender story of fourteen-year-old Sara and how her life changes when her younger, mentally challenged brother disappears. A wonderful story for families with special children.

Sharon Creech, *Bloomability.*

> A young American girl whose job-hopping father moves frequently from state to state is taken in by her uncle and aunt for a year ("kidnapped," as she puts it) to attend their

international boarding school in the Swiss Alps. There she learns about skiing, different cultures, and making lifelong friends.

Karen Cushman, *The Ballad of Lucy Whipple.*

California Morning's widowed mother uproots the family from their comfortable Massachusetts environs to settle in a rough mining camp in the Sierras, California. Her adventurous mother expects she will get over it, but California Morning writes histrionic letters to her grandparents, "I am bodaciously sorrow-burdened and wretched!" This story energizes and puts flesh on the drama of the Gold Rush years and is packed with more history than many textbooks.

Lloyd C. Douglas, *The Robe.*

The story of the Roman soldier who wins Jesus' robe from a roll of the dice at the foot of the cross. An engrossing tale of love, suspense, political intrigue, and redemption vividly set in ancient Rome.

Paula Fox, *Slave Dancer.* NM

Young Jesse suffers capture and indenture on a slave ship. There his job is to play his pipe so that the slaves will dance to get exercise and thus remain healthy until sold.

_____, *The Village by the Sea.*

Emma, visiting her uncle and aunt at a Long Island beach, spends most of her time with a new friend, constructing a village on the beach. Her aunt spoils her creation, but Emma learns a way to forgive her.

_____, *One-Eyed Cat.* NH

Ned receives a gun for his eleventh birthday but is forbidden by his parents to use it. He disobeys and believes that he shot out the eye of a wild cat and must handle his guilt. Paula Fox's books have reflective themes woven into the adventure.

Patricia Reilly Giff, *Lily's Crossing.* NH

Lily Mollahan's life is changing drastically during World War II. Her father is overseas, her best friend moves to a wartime factory town, and she meets a Hungarian refugee named Albert. Soon Lily and Albert are sharing their wishes, fears, and dreams, but they each also tell a lie, and Lily realizes that hers may cost Albert his life. It takes courage to fix our mistakes.

_____, *Nory Ryan's Song.*
> The heart-breaking tale of an Irish family during the Great
> Potato Famine in Ireland and one girl's determination to survive.

Virginia Hamilton, *M. C. Higgins, the Great.* NM
> M. C. Higgins dreams of a better life for his family in the
> Cumberland Mountains. Though his dreams seem unlikely
> to come true, the intensity of their family bonds sustain him
> through the grim tragedy of seeing strip miners spoil the
> beauty of their surroundings. Written with grace and insight.

_____, *House of Dies Drear.*
_____, *The Mystery of Drear House.*
> Absorbing tales of suspense and drama when the Small family
> senses there is something strange about this Civil War house
> that used to be a stop for the underground railway and find it
> to be the home of a once-famous abolitionist.

_____, *Anthony Burns: The Defeat and Triumph of a Fugitive Slave.*
> Within months Anthony Burns is captured in the north after
> running away from his master. A true story, this incident and
> the trial surrounding it became a turning point in the northern
> antislavery movement.

_____, *Zeely.*
> Geeder's summer at her uncle's farm is special because of a
> very tall, composed woman who looks like a Watusi queen.

_____, *Bluish.*
> Dreenie doesn't know what to make of sickly Natalie in her
> wheelchair because her skin appears blue.

Karen Hesse, *Out of the Dust.* NM
> Poetic prose to break your heart—this is a story for grown-ups
> too. Billie Jo records in her diary what happened during the
> terrible drought and dust storms of the early 1930s in the
> panhandle of Texas. "Without sod the water vanished, the soil
> turned to dust. Until the wind took it, lifting it up and carrying
> it away . . . Sorrow climbed up our front steps, big as Texas, and
> we didn't even see it coming." Fourteen and up.

_____, *Witness.*
> Using the same free verse, eleven voices relate the Ku Klux
> Klan's surprising infiltration into a small Vermont town and
> especially affects an African-American family and a Jewish girl.
> Part mystery and part social commentary, with lots to discuss.

_____, *Stowaway*.

> Nicholas Young, an eleven-year-old stowaway aboard Captain James Cook's ship *Endeavor* in the year 1768, records his adventures in his journal—one terrific yarn for readers to enjoy.

Jennifer Holm, *Our Only May Amelia*. NH

> A headstrong young girl lives with her Finnish family in a remote settlement on the coast of Oregon and copes with being the only girl in a family of seven brothers. Through many adventures, she proves herself capable of almost anything. Based on the life of the author's grandmother.

_____, *Boston Jane, An Adventure*.

> Boston-born Jane Peck, sixteen, ventures to the northwest to wed her childhood idol, William Baldt, and encounters more than she planned on.

Kimberly Willis Holt, *My Louisiana Sky*.

> Ten-year-old Tiger Ann Parker is smart. She gets straight A's and wins all the spelling contests. Her parents are mentally handicapped, and the town wonders where Tiger Ann gets her brains. Tiger loves her parents, but the community and her classmates mostly shun the whole family. Told in a southern voice in a 1950 setting, the story tells us a lot about Tiger Ann.

Phillip M. Hoose, *We Were There, Too: Young People in U.S. History*.

> Who were the young people who played an important role in our history? The stories of dozens of teens who made a difference and helped change history.

Francisco Jimenez, *The Circuit*. BG/HB

> A collection of stories based on the author's experience as a child in a migrant farmworker family. Panchito's dream is to stay in one place, to go to school without interruption, and to return to a place he recognizes. Each of these short stories builds quietly to a surprising ending. It is good to stand in another's shoes.

Lynn Joseph, *The Color of My Words*.

> A small novel about Ana Rose and her family in the Dominican Republic. Twelve-year-old Ana Rose is a poet and writer recording everything she sees, hears, and imagines. Dark shadows come into their lives when an official tells them the government

has sold their land. Seeking justice, the villagers band together, and Ana Rose's brother Guario becomes the spokesperson. An achingly beautiful book that gives new insights.

Eric P. Kelly, *The Trumpeter of Krakow.* NM
A dramatic tale of fifteenth-century Poland with a courageous young patriot, lots of tense political intrigue, and a mysterious jewel of great value. A wonderful classic written in 1929.

Rudyard Kipling, *Captains Courageous.*
A sea adventure about a spoiled American child who becomes a man while enduring some tough experiences on a voyage across the Atlantic.

Kathryn Lasky, *True North: A Novel of the Underground Railroad.*
Fourteen-year-old Lucy, daughter of a proper upperclass Boston family in 1858, finds Afrika, a young runaway slave, hiding in her grandfather's house. Their lives collide, and Lucy takes the risk of helping Afrika escape to the north. A story of courage and history.

Madeleine L'Engle, *Meet the Austins,* a series.
When Maggie Hamilton, a girl with a difficult past, comes to live with the Austins, their harmonious world is thrown into chaos. Fourteen-year-old Vicki tells this story with humor and shares the life lessons learned about change and acceptance in the context of intimate family life.
_____, *The Moon by Night.*
_____, *The Ring of Endless Light.*
_____, *Troubling a Star.*
These are the books I recommend from the series.

Gail Carson Levine, *The Wish.*
Granted one wish by an old lady on the subway, Wilma wishes to be "the most popular kid at Claverford." But, like others who have been offered one wish to come true, she finds a definite downside to the experience. The story examines what it means to be popular and what it means to be true to yourself.
_____, *Ella Enchanted.* NM
Cursed with the fairy's gift of absolute obedience, feisty Ella's life is in peril because her stepmother and two treacherous stepsisters make her life miserable. This is a most remarkable

and delightful version of a modern-day Cinderella. And yes,
she falls in love, but it is complicated!

_____, *Dave at Night*.

It's 1926 and Dave's beloved father is dead and his stepmother
doesn't want him. Only the Hebrew Home for Boys (HHB–
Hell Hole for Brats) will take Dave. Although he vows he
will escape and find a better place, it doesn't prove as easy
as he thought. Dave is no ordinary kid, and he does sneak out
regularly and returns from a whole new world he discovers
at night. In the end Dave transforms the HHB.

Hugh Lofting, *The Voyages of Dr. Doolittle*. NM

Wildly impossible and very funny adventures of a doctor who
learns animal languages. Look for others in the series. This is a
classic for older readers.

Robin McKinley, *The Hero and the Crown*. NM

In the mythical kingdom of Damar, the only daughter of the king
becomes a daring warrior, facing fire-breathing dragons and evil
wizards with courage, succeeding where all others have failed.

_____, *The Blue Sword*, a prequel.

_____, *Beauty*.

A marvelous telling of *Beauty and the Beast*. A princess named
Rosie is known more for her love of reading than for her beauty.
Imagine her delight to find that the Beast is a bookworm with a
library stocked with not only existing works, but even books not
yet written. No wonder Beauty falls for the Beast.

_____, *Spindle's End*.

A complex retelling of the *Sleeping Beauty* story.

_____, *The Outlaws of Sherwood Forest*.

McKinley deals in fairy stories for young adults.

Jean Merrill, *The Pushcart War*.

A satirical story of New York's pushcart peddlers who carry on
a guerrilla war with the traffic-clogging trucks. A simple story
about a complex subject: war. It shows how our small quarrels
are just like the "real thing."

Lucy Maud Montgomery, *Anne of Green Gables*, a series.

With her red hair, freckles, and delightful personality, Anne
Shirley has found a place in the hearts of many generations of
readers. Orphaned as an infant, eleven-year-old Anne finally finds

a real home on Prince Edward Island with Marilla and Matthew Cuthbert, and manages to enchant, shock, puzzle, and amuse the local population. It would be hard to find a dearer story.

———, *Emily of New Moon*, a series.

When Emily Starr's beloved father dies, she is sent to live with her mother's snobbish relatives at New Moon farm. Emily is sure she'll never be happy, but soon learns to deal with her stern Aunt Elizabeth and her cruel classmates. Montgomery based this trilogy on her own life.

Katherine Paterson, *Preacher's Boy.*

In Vermont at the end of the nineteenth century, preacher's son Robbie decides to become an atheist or "whatever is the most fun." The story is in the tradition of Huck Finn and Tom Sawyer. Robbie says he "ain't got the knack for holiness," but he turns out not to be very good at sinning either. Robbie finds out the importance of choices and beliefs the hard way. This finely tuned novel captures the essence of an adolescent's fundamental questions about God and existence.

———, *Jip: His Story.*

Jip is an orphan in a poorhouse farm in rural 1895 Vermont. At the home, Jip befriends a lunatic locked in a cage and changes the life of both of them. A hard, but beautiful story.

———, *Come Sing, Jimmy Jo.*

———, *Jacob Have I Loved.* NM

———, *The Master Puppeteer.*

———, *Rebels of the Heavenly Kingdom.*

———, *Park's Quest.*

Katherine Paterson's fine prose tells a good story. Her books are not always optimistic in outlook but very moving. In response, Paterson would say that is the way life is.

Richard Peck, *A Long Way from Chicago.* NH

Larger-than-life Grandma Dowdel shocks her Chicago-bred grandchildren with her ungrandmotherly ways as Joey and Mary Alice spend a week with Grandma for seven summers. Each tale about Grandma is rich in humor, verve, and substance. Armed with her twelve-gauge double-barreled rifle and her own sense of truth and justice, Grandma is full of surprises.

_____, *A Year Down Yonder.* NM

The hard-hitting Depression means that Mother and Father
have to move into one room and must send their son Joey to
his uncle and their daughter Mary Alice to Grandma Dowdel.
Mary Alice is less than thrilled about a year spent with such a
strange lady and worries about the new school she will attend.
Her dread turns into delight in one of the most exciting years
of her life. All ages.

Mary Francis Shura, *Gentle Annie.*

Anna Etheridge becomes a famous young nurse during the
Civil War. This is the story of her life leading into the war and
her service on the battlefield, a story of courage and strength.

Robert Siegel, *Whalesong Trilogy.*

Enter the world of Hruna and his son Hralekana and a pod of
humpback whales. Someone said of these books, "It is almost as
if *Moby Dick* were scaled down and rewritten from the view-
point of the whale." You will never whale-watch the same way.

_____, *White Whale.*

_____, *The Ice at the End of the World.*

William O. Steele, *The Perilous Road.* NH

A Civil War story in which two brothers choose different
loyalties. Chris Brabson is outraged when the Yankees raid their
store of winter food, their only horse, and other possessions.
When his older brother betrays this rage by joining the Union
Army, Chris's Tennessee family feels the impact of the war in
new ways.

_____, *Flaming Arrows.*

A Tennessee settlement is trapped by raiding Indians and
without a good water supply, and someone in the settlement
is suspected of being a traitor. Chad learns it is best to "think
things through" before accusing someone.

_____, *Winter Danger.*

Elizabeth George Speare, *The Bronze Bow.* NM

Daniel has hated the Romans since the death of his parents and
wants revenge. He joins a gang of ruffians, journeys back to the
city, and meets Jesus of Nazareth. One of the best books you
will read!

_____, *Calico Captive.*

>After a year's stay, a young girl captured during an Indian raid during the French and Indian War must make a choice between her old life and the life she is offered with a man who loves her.

_____, *The Witch of Blackbird Pond.* NM

>This historical novel set in Puritan Connecticut is the story of Kit, who is befriended by an old Quaker woman, Hannah Tupper, known in the village as a witch. When Hannah escapes, the blame shifts to Kit, who must defend herself against superstitious villagers.

_____, *The Sign of the Beaver.* NH

>Matt Hallowell is left on his own in a cabin in the Maine woods. Danger surrounds him at every turn until he encounters an Indian chief and his son.

Robert Louis Stevenson, *Treasure Island,* il. N. C. Wyeth.

>Everyone needs to meet Long John Silver and see the complexities of pirates. Good writing, exciting plots—who could ask for more! Look for the edition with N. C. Wyeth illustrations.

Mildred D. Taylor, *Roll of Thunder, Hear My Cry.* NM

_____, *Let the Circle Be Unbroken.*

_____, *The Road to Memphis.*

>These three stories of the Logan family in the late 1930s are powerful reading. Because of the multilayered dimensions of the story, these books should be read and talked about by young adults and parents. Mildred Taylor writes sensitively and with truthfulness. I can think of no better reading for confronting racial issues.

_____, *The Land,* a prequel to *Roll of Thunder.*

Corrie ten Boom with John Sherrill, *The Hiding Place.*

>Corrie's family hid Jews in their house during the Nazi invasion of Holland. When someone betrayed them, the family was sent off to concentration camps. Corrie and her sister Betsy ended up in the same camp. This is a story of deliverance from hatred and the ministry that followed because of growing faith in God.

Leon Walter Tillage, *Leon's Story,* il. Susan L. Roth. BG/HB

>"This small, quiet-looking book packs an emotional wallop that reverberates long after the reader has set the book aside." Those

words accompanied the Boston Globe-Horn Book award
Tillage received for his oral history of his life as a black man,
the unvarnished truth unencumbered by analysis or blame.

Mark Twain, ***The Adventures of Tom Sawyer.***
_____, *The Adventures of Huckleberry Finn.*
_____, *The Prince and the Pauper.*
_____, *A Connecticut Yankee in King Arthur's Court.*
    Classics every young American should know.

Jules Verne, ***Around the World in Eighty Days.***
_____, *Journey to the Center of the Earth.*
_____, *20,000 Leagues Under the Sea.*

Gloria Whelan, ***Miranda's Last Stand.***
    After her father's death on Little Big Horn, Miranda and her
    mother confront their own hatred for Chief Sitting Bull when
    he joins the Wild West Show and Mama threatens to quit her
    job.
_____, *Goodbye Vietnam.*
    Mai and her family trudge through the swamps of the Mekong
    Delta for a spine-tingling trip to a new life in the United States.
_____, *The Wild Berries Should Grow: The Story of a Summer.*
    A precocious fifth grader's inner transformation when she
    spends the summer at her grandparent's country cottage and
    learns to appreciate life in new ways.
_____, *A Time to Keep Silent.*
_____, *Friends.*
_____, *Forgive the River, Forgive the Sky.*
_____, *The Wanigan.*

Ruth White, ***Belle Prater's Boy.***
    Gypsy and her cousin Woodrow (Belle Prater's boy) each
    have a sorrow in their lives: Gypsy must face up to her father's
    death, and Woodrow must handle his mother's mysterious
    disappearance. The story, laced with humor and laughter, is
    a story of goodness as two children try to find themselves in
    their family's mysterious history.

T. H. White, ***The Sword in the Stone.***
    Merlyn takes a curious young boy named Wart and transforms
    him into King Arthur. A favorite with teens.

_____, *The Once and Future King.*

> This is actually four books in one (*The Sword in the Stone* is
> the first), adventures about Arthur par excellence.

Elizabeth Winthrop, *The Castle in the Attic* and sequels.

> Thirteen-year-old William doesn't want Mrs. Phillips, his
> nursemaid and friend, to leave him. He concocts a plan to hold
> her prisoner so she must stay with his family forever, but then
> must face the consequences and free her, even if it means going
> back in time to do so. A story of adventure, castles, dragons,
> and the fight for good against evil.

Kathryn Worth, *They Loved to Laugh.*

> At sixteen Martitia is left all alone when her parents die
> of typhoid fever in Virginia during the 1800s. A kindly
> Quaker, Doctor David, takes her into his home where she
> is overwhelmed by the boisterous teasing ways of his five
> big sons. Martitia eventually learns to laugh along with them,
> and also learns a lesson in love.

_____, *New Worlds for Josie.*

> Tomboy Josie and her older sister Elizabeth leave their
> Midwestern home for a year to study abroad at a fashionable
> Swiss boarding school where everyone must learn to speak
> French. Soon they realize that to be accepted by the European
> students they must learn to relate to *their* interests and
> understand that American isn't always first or best.

For a longer listing of books for teens, see *Honey for a Teen's
Heart.*

Chapter 21

Poetry Is for Pleasure

Poets put feelings into words. One boy said, "Poetry understands me, and is like a good friend I can tell everything to." Poetry simply says what it says. What a pity that poetry is often spoiled by insisting that readers find out all the hidden meanings—as if that could be done. Poet William Stafford said that poetry is like a wild animal—it can't be caged easily. It catches you before you catch it. He said, "When a poem catches you, it overwhelms, it surprises, it shakes you up. And often you can't provide any usual explanation for its power."

Poems are about enjoying language. You hear poetry and something happens to you, and it leaves you with something to taste in your mind and heart. Even if poetry is humorous, it will be a fresh look at the world. Read it aloud in your family and let it do what it will. Some poems you will like better than others, but that is allowed. Taste poetry and see if you like it. The menu varies from poem to poem.

Poems for Toddlers

Baby and toddler books have poetry galore. You will be reciting simple rhymes to them almost every time you open a book. Mother Goose rhymes from many different sources give babies the rhythm of language they need to hear.

poems for Intermediate Readers (Ages 4-12)

John Ciardi, *Doodle Soup.*
>One swallow of Doodle Soup sends the reader back for more. "Why Pigs Can't Write Poems" and "A Lesson in Manners" are among these witty poems.

_____, *You Read to Me, I'll Read to You.*

Beatrice Schenk de Regniers, *Sing a Song of Popcorn: Every Child's Book of Poems.*
>Wonderful poems with illustrations by nine Caldecott Medal artists.

Aileen Fisher, *Sing of the Earth and Sky.*
>Poems about our planet and the wonders beyond.

Simon James, *Days Like This: A Collection of Small Poems.*
>Eighteen poems by a variety of poets, all with exuberant spirit and artwork.

X. J. Kennedy and Dorothy M. Kennedy, *Talking Like the Rain: A Read-to-Me Book of Poems,* il. Jane Dyer.
_____, *Knock at a Star: A Child's Introduction to Poetry,* il. Karen Lee Baker.

Nancy Larrick, *When the Dark Comes Dancing: A Bedtime Poetry Book,* il. John Wallner.

Edward Lear, *The Complete Nonsense Book.*
_____, *The Owl and the Pussycat,* il. James Marshall.
>A winning team who give readers reasons to smile.

Dennis Lee, *Dinosaur Dinner (With a Slice of Alligator Pie),* il. Debbie Tilley.

David McCord, *Every Time I Climb a Tree,* il. Marc Simont.
>Wonderful poems and outstanding illustrations. An inviting book.

A. A. Milne, *When We Were Very Young.*
_____, *Now We Are Six.*
>Very British and memorable. "Whenever I walk in the London street, I'm ever so careful to watch my feet . . ."

Lilian Moore, *I'm Small and Other Verses.*
> Helps children explore those hard-to-articulate feelings of
> being small in a big world.

Iona and Peter Opie, *The Oxford Nursery Rhyme Book.*

Linda Yeatman, *A Child's Book of Prayers,* il. Tracey Williamson.

Poems for Ages 9–12

Scott Ellredge, *Wider Than the Sky: Poems to Grow Up With.*

Douglas Florian, *Winter Eyes.*

Robert Frost, *You Come Too: Favorite Poems for Young Readers.*

Eloise Greenfield, *For the Love of the Game,*
> il. Jan Spivey Gilchrist.

Henry W. Longfellow, *The Children's Own Longfellow.*

Mary O'Neill, *Hailstones and Halibut Bones,* il. Leonard Weisgard.
> A wonderful collection of poems about colors: "Brown is the
> smell of the Sunday roast." Expands and delights the
> imagination.

Jack Prelutsky, *The Twentieth-Century Children's Poetry Treasury,*
> il. Meilo So.
_____, *It's Raining Pigs and Noodles*, il. James Stevenson.
_____, *A Pizza the Size of the Sun*, il. James Stevenson. (ages 6–12)

Alison Sage, *Treasury of Children's Poetry.*
> Sage editor, multiple poets and illustrators.

Shel Silverstein, *Where the Sidewalk Ends.*
_____, *A Light in the Attic.*
_____, *Falling Up.*

James Stevenson, *Just Around the Corner.*
> Twenty-six short poems on everyday topics.

Richard Wilbur, *The Pig in the Spigot,* il. Otto Seibold.

Poems for All Ages

Paul Fleischman, *Joyful Noise: Poems for Two Voices*,
il. Eric Beddows. NM
Marvelous, lyrical, scored for two voices—one taking the left-hand part, the other taking the right-hand part—about the insect world. For all ages.

Donald Hall, editor, *The Oxford Illustrated Book of American Children's Poems*.
A short, but superior anthology of poems old and new. All ages.

Langston Hughes, *The Dream Keeper and Other Poems*,
il. Brian Pinkney.
A famous black poet from the Harlem Renaissance.

John Knapp, *A Pillar of Pepper*.
An out-of-the-ordinary, relevant, and clever book of rhymes about Bible stories. Knapp wrote these to help his children remember Bible stories. All ages.

Jane Kurtz, *River Friendly, River Wild*, il. by Neil Brennan.
Free-verse poems about the Red River flood of 1997 that devastated Grand Forks, North Dakota. Pictures and text catapult readers into the experience of loss and the importance of family and friends.

Nancy Larrick, *Piping Down the Valleys Wild*, il. Ellen Raskin.
A merry mix of verses for all ages.

Carl Sandburg, *Wind Song*, il. William A. Smith.
_____, *Early Moon*, il. James Daugherty.

Robert Louis Stevenson, *A Child's Garden of Verses*,
il. Tasha Tudor.

Nancy Willard, *Step Lightly: Poems for the Journey*, an anthology.

Chapter 22

Nourishing Your Children's Spiritual Life

It is my hope that every book listed in this bibliography adds something to the inner life of your children—a wider world, an appreciation of what is true, good, and beautiful, a sensitivity to human feeling, an excitement over the adventure of living. Books often speak great truths without ever mentioning God.

Beyond this, however, your children need to know how to relate to God, how he relates to them, what he has done for us, and the whole story of the birth of Jesus Christ, the purpose of his coming—the Cross and his Resurrection. These books will give you opportunities to talk about these important truths.

Well-Known and Well-Loved Bible Storybooks

Mary Batchelor, *The Children's Bible in 365 Stories.*
> This is my favorite Bible storybook. The stories are accurate, brief, and written in excellent prose. It's just right for ages 4–12. A good book to help establish family Bible reading.

Karyn Henley, *The Beginner's Bible,* il. Dennas Davis.
> Written at second-grade level for kids to read on their own.

Jesse L. Hurlbut, *The Complete Book of Bible Stories.*
> A long-time favorite for older readers.

Marian M. Schoolland, *Leading Little Ones to God: A Child's Book of Bible Teaching.*
> This book has been used to teach generations of children. Still in print.

Ken Taylor, *The Book for Children,* il. Richard and Frances Hook.
> Ages 4–8.

_____, *The Bible in Pictures for Little Eyes.*

Catherine Vos, *The Child's Bible Story.*
> First published sixty years ago and still going. For all ages.

More Books for Christian Understanding

Ashley Bryan, *How God Fixed Jonah.*
> Ashley Bryan has done a retelling of Lorenz Graham's African-American sermons with wonderful block prints. Not your usual Bible story, but well worth looking at and listening while it is read aloud. His story of Noah, for example, is called "God Wash the World and Start Again." Ages 9–14.

Nick Butterworth, *Stories Jesus Told,* il. Mick Inkpen.
> A series of books that little children love that retell parables and Bible stories, many through the eyes of animals.

Nancy White Carlstrom, ***Does God Know How to Tie Shoes?***
il. Lori McElrath-Eslick.

Using the book of Psalms, Carlstrom takes children's questions about God seriously. An encouragement for parents in answering such queries.

_____, *How Does the Wind Walk?*

_____, Jesse Bear series. Ages 4–8.

Kathryn Cave, ***Henry's Song,*** il. Sue Hendra.

When Henry sings for joy, the other animals complain until the Maker of All Things shows them that everyone's voice is needed to make a song. A fun story book about what God expects of us. Ages 4–8.

Rachel Field, ***Prayer for a Child,*** il. E. Jones. **CM**

A classic. Ages 4–12.

Nikki Grimes, ***At Break of Day,*** il. Paul Morin.

A vigorous and colorful retelling of the Creation story. Ages 4–8.

_____, *Come Sunday*, a funny and reverent book for introducing children to church life.

Nan Gurley, ***Twice Yours, A Parable of God's Gift,***
il. Bill Farnsworth.

A gentle story of a grandfather telling his grandson the story of a boat he once made for himself. When he lost the boat, he bought it back again. The grandfather applies this to what God has done for us. Ages 4–10.

Helen Haidle, ***Thank You, Dear God,*** il. Susan Banta.

_____, *God Bless Me.*

_____, *What Did Jesus Say and Do?* Ages 2–5.

Wendy Anderson Halperin, ***Love Is.***

A beautiful book based on 1 Corinthians 13. All ages.

Liz Curtis Higgs, ***Go Away Dark Night,*** il. Nancy Munger.

Ages 2–5.

Dave and Neta Jackson, ***Hero Tales.***

Fifteen stories of Christian heroes. Ages 6–10.

BG/HB	Boston Globe/Horn Book award
CM	Caldecott Medal
CH	Caldecott Honor
CSK	Coretta Scott King award
NA	Newbery Award
NH	Newbery Honor
NM	Newbery Medal

Matt and Lisa Jacobson, *The Amazing Beginning of You.*
>   A fascinating look at the story of birth, with real-life photos
>   for ages 8–12.

_____, *How Did God Make Me?*

Virginia Kroll, *I Wanted to Know All About God,* il. Debra Reid
Jenkins.
>   In simple yet eloquent language, this book explores a child's
>   questions about God. Ages 4–10.

Tim Ladwig, *Psalm Twenty-Three.*
>   Two glowing African-American children experience this psalm
>   in an urban neighborhood. Ages 9–12.

Elsie Larson, *Bombus the Bumblebee,* il. Elizabeth and David
Haidle.
>   A story of the gifts God gives to bumblebees. Ages 4–8.

Bijou Le Tord, *Sing a New Song, A Book of Psalms.*
_____, *God's Little Seeds, a Book of Parables.* Ages 4–8.

Paul Little, *Know Why You Believe.*
_____, *Know What You Believe.*
>   Thoughtful answers to some difficult questions. Books for a
>   thinking young person. Young adult.

Max Lucado, *Tell Me the Story,* il. Ron Dicianni.
_____, *Tell Me the Secrets.*
_____, *You Are Special.* Ages 4–8.

David R. Mains and Karen B. Mains, *Tales of the Kingdom.*
>   The story of Hero, Little Child, and Princess Amanda and their
>   relationship to the King. A trilogy of highly readable allegories
>   that point to the King and provide many ideas for discussion
>   with the family. Ages 10–12.

_____, *Tales of the Resistance.*
_____, *Tales of the Restoration.*

Rick Osborne and K. Christie Bowler, *Who Is Sam Harrington?*
il. Dara Goldman
>   All over town children are doing nice things because "It's what
>   Sam Harrington would do!" Ages 4–8.

Artwork by Sergio Martinez. Taken from *You Are Special* by Max Lucado, copyright © 1997.
Used by permission of Good News Publishers, Crossway Books, Wheaton Illinois 60187.
For more information, contact Crossway Books at 1-800-635-7993.

Leslie Parrott, *God Made You Nose to Toes,* il. Valeria Petrone.
Ages 4–8.

John and Katherine Paterson, *Images of God,*
il. Alexander Koshkin.
A collection of thoughtful interpretations of Bible readings,
illustrating how God uses everyday images to reveal his
message to his people. Striking illustrations. Ages 10 and up.

Katherine Paterson, *Who Am I?* il. Stephanie Milsnowski.
A wonderful book to talk about by an award-winning author.
A strong statement on personal worth. Ages 9–12.

Beatrice Schenk de Regniers, *David and Goliath,*
il. Scott Cameron. Ages 4–8.

Gary D. Schmidt, *The Blessing of the Lord,* il. Dennis Nolan.
Stories from the Old and New Testament. Ages 8–12.

Anne Elizabeth Stickney, *The Loving Arms of God,* il. Helen Cann.
Bible stories about how God cares for his people. Ages 6–10.

Nancy Sweetland, *God's Quiet Things,* il. Rick Stevens.
A child's invitation to explore the quiet wonders in God's
creation. Ages 4–8.

Helen L. Taylor, *Little Pilgrim's Progress.*
Simplified version of the famous Bunyan classic that captures
the essence of its spiritual truths without writing "down" to
children. Ages 8–12.

Paul White, *Jungle Doctor Fables.*
Like Aesop, missionary doctor Paul White uses animal stories to
teach lessons and delight readers. Told with the skill and flavor
of a master African storyteller, these books appeal to all ages.
_____, *Jungle Doctor Cartoon Collection.*
This may get non-book kids into reading while teaching them
at the same time. These books originate in Australia and may
be hard to find, but can be ordered through a bookstore.

Brian Wildsmith, *Exodus.*
_____, *Joseph.*
With Wildsmith's marvelous artwork, these stories come alive
in new ways. Ages 9–12.

Chapter 23

A Book List
for Special Occasions

I'm frequently asked for ideas for special occasions that are not on the normal book list. The four most common requests: (1) books on facing grief and loss, (2) Christmas stories, (3) Easter stories, and (4) Thanksgiving stories. This chapter contains book suggestions for these four areas of life.

Stories about Grieving and Loss

I find this the most difficult category for a book list. Death is a terribly hard reality. Little children can scarcely grasp its permanence. No matter what your age, it's a tough subject. In recent years more writers have attempted to grapple with ways to help children facing the loss of people they love. I have included a list of books that deal with loss, creative ways to help children understand and talk about their feelings. It is not enough; we need more books on this subject, but it is a good beginning. In the end, we rely on God's grace to comfort and take us beyond our limited understanding, but I hope some of these books will help.

When I was collecting these books I couldn't help thinking that Christmas and Easter are the best news in the world in the face of death and suffering! When Joni Eareckson lay on a hospital bed contemplating the news that she was now a quadriplegic at seventeen, following a diving accident, one of her friends appeared in her room after hours, lay on her bed, put her arms around Joni, and simply sang *When I Survey the Wondrous Cross*. Joni said that no other words spoken in sympathy helped her cope with what she was facing as much as the fact of Jesus' death and resurrection. It helps to have a God who knows about suffering.

Taken from *Papa's Gift* by Kathleen Bostrom.
Illustrated by Guy Porfirio. Copyright © 2002 by Kathleen Bostrom.
Illustrations copyright © 2002 by Guy Porfirio. Used by permission of Zondervan.

Mary Bahr, *If Nathan Were Here,* il. Karen A. Jerome.
> This books gently touches the grieving that comes when a child loses a peer. Ages 5–10.

Kathleen Bostrom, *Papa's Gift,* il. Guy Porfirio.
> A beautiful story of the friendship of a grandfather and granddaughter and their adventures together. When Papa dies, little Clara refuses to be comforted, until she remembers what he had told her and sees with new eyes. The wonderful illustrations alone are comforting. All ages.

Nancy White Carlstrom, *Blow Me a Kiss, Miss Lilly,* il. Amy Schwartz.
> Sara's best friend is Miss Lilly, who is very old. They blow kisses to each other right to the end. Ages 4–10.

Lucille Clifton, *Everett Anderson's Goodbye,* il. Ann Grifalconi.
> A lovely book. A poetic telling of Everett Anderson's feelings as he copes with grief and accepts his father's death. The book takes you gently through the stages of grieving. All ages.

Dave Dravecky, *Dave Dravecky.*
> A first-class pitcher in the big leagues loses his arm to cancer. From the Today's Heroes series for ages 8–12.

Mary Joslin, *The Goodbye Boat,* il. Claire St. Louis Little.
> Saying goodbye when someone you love dies is perhaps the hardest thing of all. This book provides a message of hope that sadness will ease and that death is not the end. Ages 5–10.

Eiko Kadono, *Grandpa's Soup,* il. Satomi Ichikawa.
> Grandpa discovers that sharing with friends is the best cure for loneliness after his sadness over Grandma's death. Ages 5–10.

Gregg Lewis and Deborah S. Lewis, *Today's Heroes: Joni Eareckson Tada.*
> A seventeen-year-old girl faces life as a quadriplegic. Inspiring. Ages 12 and up.

Larry Libby, *Someday Heaven,* il. Wayne McLoughlin.
> Thoughtful, comforting, Scripture-based answers to common questions children ask about heaven and what happens at death. All ages.

Katherine Paterson, *The Bridge to Terabithia.* NM
> Jess and Leslie, best friends, share a secret kingdom named Terabithia they have created in the woods. When Leslie dies, Jess must face his terrible loss and learn how to go on. Ages 9–12.

June R. Thomas, *Saying Goodbye to Grandma,* il. Marcia Sewall.
> Seven-year-old Susie is curious and fearful about what Grandmother's funeral will be like. A soft, nonthreatening look at death. Ages 7–12.

Barbara J. Turner, *A Little Bit of Rob,* il. Marni Backer.
> Almost everything reminds the family of their brother Rob. They miss him from the moment they step into the boat on their crabbing expedition. A book about how memories help us in grieving. Ages 5–10.

Susan Varley, *Badger's Parting Gifts.*
> All the woodland creatures mourn when old Badger dies. A beautiful book about sharing memories in your loss. All ages.

Gloria Whelan, *Forgive the River, Forgive the Sky.*
> A young girl struggles with loss and forgiveness when her father dies.

_____, *A Time to Keep Silent.*
> When her mother dies, thirteen-year-old Clair stops talking to get her father's attention. Young adult.

Charlotte Zolotow, *My Grandson Lew,* il. William Pene Du Bois.
> You may need to get this quiet and thoughtful book from the library. All ages.

Christmas Stories

With the secularization of religious holidays, families want to be intentional about emphasizing the real meaning of these celebrations. Seuss's *How the Grinch Stole Christmas* reminds us to do that.

> *Then the Grinch thought of something he hadn't before!*
> *"Maybe Christmas," he thought, "doesn't come from a store.*
> *Maybe Christmas perhaps means a little bit more!"*

It is also more than a sweet look at a baby born in a manger. Christmas is the ultimate love story. It is the story of God invading human history in the person of Jesus. What a mind-expanding concept! It may take years for your children to comprehend its significance.

Beautiful books that tell the real meaning of Christmas ought to be part of your decorations at Christmas time. Along with those that tell about the birth of Jesus are others that are sweet stories—good for the heart, but not necessarily about Jesus. You can tell from the annotations which tell The Story and which are about the spirit of love and generosity that characterizes Christmas.

Because we are all children at Christmas, a good Christmas story has an ageless appeal.

Inos Biffi, ***The Way to Bethlehem,*** il. Franco Vignazia.

Margaret Wise Brown, ***A Child Is Born,*** il. Floyd Cooper.
    A lovely telling of that wonderful night for little people.

Rebecca Caudill, ***A Certain Small Shepherd.***
    A sweet story for small children that has been in print a long time.

Anne Dixon, ***Waiting for Noel, an Advent Story,*** il. Mark Graham.
    Noel's family lights the advent candles to celebrate.

Margery Facklam, ***Only a Star,*** il. Nancy Carpenter.
    What were the decorations that first Christmas night?

Ruth Bell Graham, ***One Wintry Night,*** il. Richard Jesse Watson.

Margaret Hodges, ***Silent Night: The Song and Its Story,***
    il. Tim Ladwig.
        Wonderful illustrations.

Angela Elwell Hunt, *The Tale of Three Trees*, il. Tim Jonke.
Traditional folktale retold.

Ezra Jack Keats, *The Little Drummer Boy*.
Christmas season, not specifically biblical.

Astrid Lindgren, *Pippi Longstocking's After-Christmas Party*, il. Michael Chesworth.
Christmas seasonal, not religious.

Max Lucado, *The Crippled Lamb*, il. Liz Bonham.
Lucado always has the right touch for the heart.
_____, *Alabaster's Song: Christmas Through the Eyes of an Angel*.
An alabaster angel on the Christmas tree transports a little boy back to the first Christmas, a charming story that teaches that Christmas is more than presents and trees.

Alan MacDonald, *The Not-So-Wise Man*, il. Andrew Rowland.
Another wise man named Ashtar keeps missing the most important things of all.

Trinka Hakes Noble, *Apple Tree Christmas*.
A gentle story of a girl whose love for an old apple tree changes her Christmas. Seasonal.

Mary Quattlebaum, *The Shine Man*, il. Tim Ludwig.
An allegory. "What you do for the least of these brothers of mine, you do for me."

Michael J. Rosen, *Elijah's Angel*, il. Aminah Brenda Lynn Robinson.
An African-American barber befriends a small Jewish boy and they share the meaning of Christmas and Chanukah. Based on a true story.

Charles M. Schulz, *A Charlie Brown Christmas*.
Seasonal, not specifically religious, fun.

Julie Vivas, *The Nativity*.
You have never imagined the Christmas story as Vivas' lively pictures tell it!

Lori Walburg, *The Legend of the Candy Cane*, il. James Bernardin.
A charming story of a candy storeowner and a small girl who spread the word about the meaning of the candy cane and thus tell the real story of Christmas.

Walter Wangerin Jr., *Mary's First Christmas,* il. Timothy Ladwig.
> Mary retells the story of the first Christmas to the young boy Jesus. Lovely illustrations.

Gloria Whelan, *The Miracle of St. Nicholas,* il. Judith Brown.
> A touching story of endurance of faith in a Russian village where the church's treasures miraculously appear on Christmas morning after the church has been closed by soldiers for sixty years. A religious story.

Brian Wildsmith, *A Christmas Story.*
> Young Rebecca and a little donkey follow Mary and Joseph to Bethlehem.

Susan Wojciechowski, *The Christmas Miracle of Jonathan Toomey,* il. P.J. Lynch.
> A boy and his mother change the life of an embittered wood-carver when they ask him to make new figures for their créche.

Taken from *The Legend of the Candy Cane* by Lori Walburg.
Illustrated by James Bernardin. Copyright © 1997 by Zondervan. Illustrations
copyright © 1997 by James Bernardin. Used by permission of Zondervan.

Easter Stories

Easter is the most important day on the Christian calendar. More than chocolate eggs, children need to encounter the wonder of the risen Christ. It is the validation of Christian faith! As a child matures and reaches new levels of understanding, don't assume they know the reason for the death of Jesus. One middle school student, familiar with the Bible from both home and Sunday school, honestly wrote, "Why did God let those wicked men kill his own Son? It seems so unfair." The answer to that question holds the key to what being a Christian is all about. Help children understand the meaning of his death and that the resurrection of Jesus is so important that we celebrate it every Sunday.

Melody Carlson, *Benjamin's Box,* il. Jack Stockman.
> The story of Benjamin's encounters with Jesus and his experience of sadness when he is crucified and later the joy of his resurrection. Ages 5–10.

Lloyd Douglas, *The Robe.*
> An Easter classic about the man who gambled for Christ's robe and won. Ages 12 and up. A good family read-aloud book for Easter time.

Helen Haidle, *Journey to the Cross,* il. David and Paul Haidle.
> The complete Easter story for young readers.

_____, *He Is Alive.*
> A picture book for ages 4–8.

Harold L. Myra, *Easter Bunny, Are You for Real?* il. Jane Kurisu.
> An interesting story that takes a child from the Easter bunny to the real meaning of Easter. Ages 4–8.

Lori Walburg, *The Legend of the Easter Egg,* il. James Bernardin. Ages 5–10.
> How does the tradition of Easter eggs fit in with the story of the Resurrection?

Walter Wangerin Jr., *Peter's First Easter,* il. Timothy Ladwig.
> Beautifully illustrated, a wonderful look at Easter from Peter's point of view. All ages.

Brian Wildsmith, *The Easter Story.*
> Wildsmith's bold strokes tell the story with splendor.

Taken from *Peter's First Easter* by Walter Wangerin Jr.
Illustrated by Timothy Ladwig. Copyright © 2000 by Walter Wangerin Jr.
Illustrations copyright © 2000 by Timothy Ladwig.
Used by permission of Zondervan.

Thanksgiving Stories

One last category: Increasingly the Thanksgiving holiday is becoming the time when the extended family gathers. More than a day of remembrance, it calls for a spirit of thankfulness to be nurtured. Thanksgiving was not, as is sometimes said in schools, the pilgrims thanking the Indians; it was a thanksgiving to God. Our celebration should be more than "turkey day," a day for overeating, with little conversation about the truth of its history or significance in family life. I have listed some Thanksgiving books for your library, for active use each year when this holiday comes around. I was impressed with how many of these stories deal with being thankful in the face of loss.

Louisa May Alcott, *An Old-Fashioned Thankgiving*.
> The seven rambunctious Bassett children decide to cook their own Thanksgiving dinner after their parents leave to tend a sick grandmother. Minor catastrophes and understandable chaos add to the charm of this rediscovered family classic. It is sentimental and perfect for the holiday.

Eve Bunting, *How Many Days to America: A Thanksgiving Story*, il. Beth Peck.
> The story of contemporary pilgrims leaving what is familiar with some of the same fears and hardships the early pilgrims faced. Ages 4–8.

Barbara Cohen, *Molly's Pilgrim*, il. Daniel M. Duffy.
> A young Jewish immigrant tells her friends the story of Thanksgiving, and they learn that it takes all kinds of pilgrims to make Thanksgiving. Ages 5–10.

Alice Dalgleish, *The Thanksgiving Story*, il. Marcia Sewall. CH

James Daugherty, *The Landing of the Pilgrims*.
> The story told by a Newbery medal author. Ages 9–12.

Barbara Greenwood, *A Pioneer Story*, il. Heather Collins.
_____, *A Pioneer Thanksgiving: A Story of Harvest Celebrations in 1841.*
> A weaving together of stories, information, and activities to create a tapestry of pioneer life. Wonderful illustrations, great family book. All ages.

Helen Haidle, ***Thank You, Dear God!*** il. Susan Banta.

A board book for little children about things to be thankful for.

B. G. Hennesy, ***One Little, Two Little, Three Little Pilgrims,***
il. Lynne Cravath.

A thanksgiving book for two- and three-year-olds.

Anna Kamma, ***If You Were at the First Thanksgiving,***
il. Bert Dodson.

The historical details of the first Thanksgiving in Plymouth.

Verla Kay, ***Tattered Sails,*** il. Dan Andreasen.

A pilgrim family journeys across the ocean and comes to
freedom in America.

Patricia Lakin, ***Fat Chance Thanksgiving,*** il. Stacey Schuett.

A lonely girl, newcomer to a housing project, decides to get
everyone in the building together for Thanksgiving, getting
at the heart of thankfulness.

Julian Scheer, ***A Thanksgiving Turkey,*** il. Ronald Himler.

Gorgeous illustrations in a story about a boy and his grandfather who hope to shoot a wild turkey in the woods, and then
deliberately miss the shot. A wonderfully tender story about
youth and old age.

Gary D. Schmidt, ***William Bradford: Plymouth's Faithful Pilgrim.***

A biography of the Colony's major character as he tries to be
fair to the pilgrims and the native Americans.

Margaret Walley, ***Thanksgiving with Me,*** il. Lloyd Bloom.

A beautifully illustrated celebration story of a little girl who
cannot wait for her beloved uncles to arrive for Thanksgiving
Day.

Index of Authors

Index of Book Titles

Honey for a teen's heart

Using Books to Communicate with Teens

Gladys Hunt

Getting excited about what books can do is contagious, and so is the reading habit!

This book inspires reading, but it does more. It shows you how to use books to communicate with the teens in your family to help them build a truly Christian world/life view. Families need to talk together, to listen to each other, to ask questions about truth, to discover together what makes life sing with meaning. *Honey for a Teen's Heart* offers practical advice about how to read, what to read, what to look for in a book. Gladys Hunt is clearly out to help you influence your teen in a way that signals growth and thoughtfulness. She has a way of making you want to read, while giving you clues that help you find the significance of a book. Hurrah for books that widen our world and give so much pleasure at the same time.

To help you choose what to read, Barbara Hampton has annotated more than 350 titles, a third of them from the last decade. Recommendations range from classics like *A Tale of Two Cities* to contemporary fiction like *A Ring of Endless Light;* from literary greats like J. R. R. Tolkien and Chaim Potok to moderns like Katherine Paterson and Sharon Creech; from books just for fun like *Ella Enchanted* to thoughtful explorations of our values like *Eva.* They will take you around the world, across time and back as a richer family.

This books contains

- Ideas for building family life by reading together
- Ways to use books to talk about values with teens
- Advice to use books to cope with culture
- Ways to help your teen think Christianly
- Hundreds of book ideas to explore and the right questions to ask
- Tips for getting ready for college
- A complete index to authors and titles

Softcover 0-310-24260-6

Pick up a copy today at your favorite bookstore!

ZONDERVAN™

GRAND RAPIDS, MICHIGAN 49530 USA

WWW.ZONDERVAN.COM

Honey for a *Woman's Heart*

Growing Your World through Reading Great Books

Gladys Hunt

Gladys Hunt, long-time advocate of reading and author of the cherished *Honey for a Child's Heart*, has written this book for busy women who want a wider worldview and stimulus for intellectual and emotional growth. *Honey for a Woman's Heart* explores

- The wonder of words, language, and reading
- What good books offer thoughtful readers
- What makes a good book
- The value of reading fiction
- Best books in genres of fiction, nonfiction, spirituality, and poetry
- How to enjoy the best of books: the Bible
- The pleasure of sharing books with others
- Something for everyone, no matter what age or reading experience
- Recommendations for over 500 books to enjoy

Pleasant words are a honeycomb, sweet to the soul and healing to the bones.
PROVERBS 16:24

Softcover 0-310-23846-3

Pick up a copy today at your favorite bookstore!

ZONDERVAN™

GRAND RAPIDS, MICHIGAN 49530 USA

WWW.ZONDERVAN.COM

We want to hear from you. Please send your comments about this
book to us in care of the address below. Thank you.

GRAND RAPIDS, MICHIGAN 49530 USA

WWW.ZONDERVAN.COM